Navigating Britain's Coastline
Portland to Dover

Adrienne & Peter Oldale

David & Charles

Newton Abbot   London   North Pomfret (Vt)

Navigating Britain's coastline
  2: Portland to Dover
  1. Pilot guides - Great Britain
  2. Coastwise navigation - Great Britain
  3. Great Britain - Description and travel -
  1971 - Views
  I. Oldale, Adrienne   II. Oldale, Peter
  623.89'29'41   VK827
ISBN 0-7153-7934-8
Library of Congress Catalog Card Number 80-68901
© Adrienne and Peter Oldale 1981
Typeset by Photoprint, Paignton and
printed in Great Britain
by A. Wheaton & Co. Ltd., Hennock Road, Exeter, Devon
for David & Charles (Publishers) Limited
Brunel House Newton Abbot Devon
Published in the United States of America
by David & Charles Inc
North Pomfret Vermont 05053 USA

Great care has been taken in the preparation of this book, but the authors
and publishers regret that they cannot be held responsible for damage or
inconvenience caused by any error or omission that might remain. The
authors would be pleased to hear the views of users.

Acknowledgements

In producing this book we have received assistance and advice from many
sources. We would like to acknowledge this help with gratitude. In particular
we thank the officers of the coastguard service who have assisted us in so
many ways with unfailing skill and courtesy.

We thank too the staff and masters of the harbours along the coast, in
particular the Dover Harbour Patrol and control officers.

Finally, our thanks to the many seagoing friends who have encouraged us
in what turned out to be a more difficult undertaking than we expected!

Coastguards

At various places we have indicated the presence of particularly conspicuous
coastguard buildings. There are however, very many others from which
lookout is kept from time to time.

Introduction

This volume, the second we have published of its type, completes our visual
survey of the entire south coast of England. Our previous book covered the
stretch from Land's End to Portland Bill; the present one the whole coast
between Portland and the South Foreland, just east of Dover.

The plan of the books arose from our own needs, discovered when we first
began to sail extensively along unfamiliar coasts. It was then a constant
problem to work out precisely where we were. On the chart we could see
many objects marked 'conspic' — churches, hills, islands, headlands, etc —
but it was not always easy to identify them on the shore. The churches
seemed mostly to be buried in trees, there were often three or four similar
hills, islands seemed to be part of the mainland, headlands looked like islands
. . .

What we needed was some local seaman, familiar with the coastline, to
point and say: 'That cliff there — that's Worbarrow and you can just see the
Lulworth Cove entry over to the left.' At the same time he might put his
finger on the correct place on our chart. This book aims to give just such
help.

Three years ago we decided to make a guide to the coast by producing a
book of 'views' that would show the whole coastline from a distance of a
mile or two off. Under each view we would write useful information. Besides
giving the shape and general aspect of the shore, we would also add
enlargements of special items such as beacons, churches, lighthouses and so
on. Finally, we would supply a simple outline 'chartlet' to aid in locating
these items on your navigation chart.

We rapidly found we had taken on a big job. To produce these first two
volumes we have sailed some three thousand miles and taken literally
hundreds of photographs. Every page is based on such photos, taken from
positions plotted by radar, and chosen to give a fair idea of the coast's
appearance from close in — between ½ mile and 1½ miles as a rule. English
Channel weather being what it is, there were days and weeks when no
useful photography could be done. We would sail back and forth along a
section of coastline peering out through the drizzling rain, creeping mist or
blue heat-haze, vainly trying to pick out a particular hill we were assured was
'conspic' or 'easy to distinguish'. Coasts that faced westwards could not be
photographed in the mornings. Coasts that faced eastwards could not be
photographed in the afternoon. In choppy conditions considerable agility was
required to hold a camera steady.

At last the photographs were taken, and all of them were then combined
to give a consistent series of views that could be carefully drawn to scale.
Nothing is shown on the views unless we have actually seen it ourselves.
Besides charted navigational objects, we also discovered items that were not
charted, in particular the now ubiquitous caravan parks which are remarkably

visible for long distances at sea, and these too we have included on our drawings.

This introduced the question of what exactly a navigational mark was — how it could be judged and described. We found, as we sailed along, many charted marks that could barely be seen, and if seen could not be identified for certain. Moreover, even those that could be so identified were not always of any actual use. The outcome of our thoughts was the 'VIU' (view) code described below. With this, navigation marks can be graded according to their three main characteristics — their VISIBILITY, IDENTIFIABILITY and UTILITY. This code is still at an early stage of development but we hope it will prove of use in making a rapid and *rational* assessment of a landmark seen, perhaps under stress, by an anxious navigator!

Now that the volumes are finished, we hope you will find them useful and welcome guides. It is impossible to imagine that, over such a long stretch of coastline, we have not made one or two mistakes, but we trust there are no major ones.

These books are not, of course, substitutes for careful navigation. The 'charts' are simply outlines of the coast, intended to help you find the particular stretch of coastline illustrated in the view. We do hope, though, that they will help you to identify the features of the coast as you pass along, not only making it easier to keep track of your position, but also adding further interest and enjoyment to voyages.

Classifying Landmarks with the 'VIU' Code

Any object on the coast used as a navigational mark must have three characteristics:
  a It must be VISIBLE
  b It must be IDENTIFIABLE
  c It must be USEFUL

There are many charted marks that are easily seen but that cannot be identified with certainty and others that are easy to identify but not easy to pick out. There are yet more that, though easy to see and identify, are of no real use to navigators, perhaps because of the presence nearby of still better marks.

At one end of the scale might be the Eddystone lighthouse. This is eminently visible, unmistakably identifiable, and extremely useful as a major 'fix' or landfall mark. Near the other end of the scale might be some small church, half concealed in trees up an obscure creek. This might only be visible at close range, be identifiable only by a local resident, and be useful only on rare occasions. On many charts, indeed, are items that are virtually invisible, cannot be identified and are of no use — most of the churches in Brighton, for instance.

On our views in this book, features are graded in a code we call the 'VIEW' or 'VIU' code, with grades from A to E in each quality:
  V — visibility
  I — identifiability
  U — utility
The grades are as follows:

VISIBILITY — given first

Grade	Meaning
A	Outstandingly visible from all seaward directions.
B	Visible clearly from most seaward directions, but view restricted from some angles or on close approach to high intervening land.
C	Not always clearly visible due to the nature, colour or shape of the mark, atmospheric pollution or confusing associated objects.
D	Visible only over a limited arc or at close range.
E	Not visible at any useful seaward distance.

IDENTIFIABILITY — given second

A	Easily identified in isolation, even by a stranger.
B	Identifiable in isolation if seen before by the observer, or by a stranger in conjunction with other data.
C	Identifiable only in conjunction with other data.
D	Difficult to identify except at close range and with local knowledge.
E	Not identifiable with certainty, or liable to change in appearance.

UTILITY — given third

A	A prime mark, usable alone as a landfall, for important 'fixes', course changes, etc.
B	A good mark usually used in conjunction with others for 'fixes', transits, clearance bearings, etc.
C	A limited mark used mainly in conjunction with a B mark. Not suitable for use alone.
D	A local mark, useful within a restricted area and always with caution or local knowledge.
E	Not of navigational use due to presence of better marks in visual range, liability to change in position, or other sources of error.

The VIU code enables the navigator to assess rapidly, bearing in mind his own estimated position, whether he is likely to be able to see a mark, to identify it if seen, and whether it will benefit him to do so!

Note: The VIU code copyright is owned by the authors. It is being studied experimentally by the Admiralty Hydrographic Department to assess its possible use in charts and sailing directions.

How to use this book

1 Every page contains at least one 'view' of a portion of the coast between the Portland peninsula and the South Foreland lighthouse. These have been prepared from specially taken photographs to give a complete picture of the main coastal features, landmarks, navigational marks, lights and harbours.

2 Below each view we give essential information about the places shown and their VIU codes (see page 3) with short vertical lines indicating their positions on the view. Where necessary to save space, the usual nautical abbreviations are used.

3 Where the wording refers to something not visible on the view the lines are dashed.

4 The descending lines lead to the objects' positions on an outline chart drawn below. Each line ends in a square except in the case of navigational lights which are marked by a hexagon.

5 THESE CHARTS ARE ONLY FOR IDENTIFICATION, TO HELP YOU FIND THE OBJECTS ON YOUR NAVIGATIONAL CHARTS. Scale approx 25mm = 1 nautical mile.

6 Towns and villages are marked by larger squares: their names are given in CAPITALS.

7 Each chart has one or more 'eyes' drawn nearby. The circle marks the place from which the view was taken. The radial lines indicate its angular extent. A row of such eyes side by side indicates that the view above is a composite of a series of overlapping pictures.

8 Blue lines are drawn along the shoreline of each view, and round the corresponding sector of the coastline on the chart below.

9 On some pages two views are given, one above the other. Each has its own information written below. Lines from the top view are simply broken where they pass the bottom view. Where some object is visible in both views, a single line may connect the two with the chart below, but the written name will then be given under both views. The 'eye' for the upper view is marked TOP.

10 Further details, such as sectors of lights, harbour approaches, enlarged views of navigational marks, are inserted at convenient places on the pages.

11 NORTH is always UP unless a printed compass rose shows a different direction.

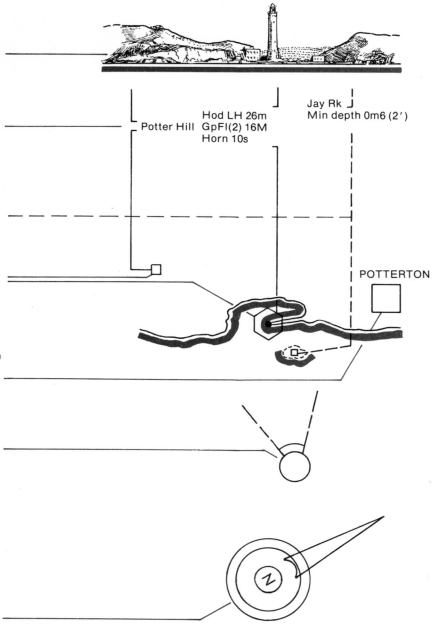

Potter Hill

Hod LH 26m
GpFl(2) 16M
Horn 10s

Jay Rk
Min depth 0m6 (2')

POTTERTON

Comment utiliser cet livre

1 Chaque page contient au moins une 'vue' d'une partie de la côte anglaise depuis la peninsule de Portland jusqu'au phare de South Foreland. Les vues ont été fondées sur des centaines de photos et montrent justement les traits de la côte, ses rochers, ses falaises, ses phares, ses ports etc.

2 Sous chaque vue nous donnons l'information essentielle sur les choses importantes qu'on peut y voir y compris le indicatif littéral VIU (voyez p 3). Des lignes verticales montrent ces positions exactes. (Nous utilisons les abbréviations maritimes.)

3 En ce qui concerne les choses qui ne sont pas visibles sur la vue, les lignes sont interrompues.

4 Les lignes descendantes montrent les positions des objets sur une carte maritime simplifiée, imprimée sous la vue. Au bout de chaque ligne on trouve un carré; pour indiquer les phares, un hexagone.

5 DANGER! Utilisez les cartes SEULEMENT POUR IDENTIFIER LES OBJETS, afin de pouvoir les trouver sur vos cartes maritimes. Echelle approximative: 25mm = 1 mille marin.

6 Les villes et les villages sont identifiés avec des carrés plus grands. Leurs noms sont imprimés en CAPITALES.

7 Sur chaque carte on remarque des 'points de vue' dont le cercle est placé exactement où nous avons pris la photo sur laquelle cette vue fut fondée. Les lignes radiales indiquent les limites angulaires de la vue. (S'il y a plusieurs des 'points de vue', la vue est composée de plusieurs photos combinées.)

8 Les lignes bleues imprimées sous les vues et sur les cartes correspondent entre elles.

9 Sur certaines pages il y a deux vues, l'une au-dessus de l'autre. L'information pour chacune est imprimée au-dessous. Les lignes verticales de la vue supérieure sont interrompues par la vue inférieure. Si un objet est visible sur toutes les deux, le nom de l'objet est imprimé sous chacune entre elles. Les points de vue supérieurs sont representés par la marque 'TOP'.

10 L'information plus détaillée (par example, les détails à propos des phares importants et de la façon de s'approcher des ports) est imprimée sur les cartes dans les endroits appropriés.

11 Le NORD est vers le haut de la page, sauf quand on trouve sur la carte une rose de vents qui est orientée dans une direction différente.

Gebrauchsanweisung

1 Auf jeder Seite dieses Buches ist mindestens eine Teilansicht der Küste zwischen dem Leuchtturm von South Foreland und der Halbinsel Portland dargestellt. Diese Ansichten basieren auf Fotografien, die extra dafür angefertigt wurden, um ein vollständiges Bild der Gesamtküste mit ihren Landmarken, Seezeichen, Leuchtfeuern und Häfen zu geben.

2 Unter jeder Ansicht geben wir Erläuterungshinweise zu den jeweils dort vorhandenen Landmarken, Seezeichen usw und ihr VIU Flaggensignalsystem (Seite 3). Ihre Position in der Ansicht wird mit kurzen vertikalen Linien dargestellt. Aus Platzgründen werden die üblichen nautischen Abkürzungen verwendet.

3 Wo sich die Erläuterungen auf solche Dinge beziehen, die in der Ansicht nicht sichtbar sind, ist die Linie gestrichelt.

4 Eine Verbindungslinie zeigt die entsprechende Position durch ein Viereck im Seekartenausschnitt an, der unter der jeweiligen Ansicht angedeutet ist. Bei Leuchtfeuern werden Sechsecke verwendet.

5 ACHTUNG: diese Kartenskizzen sind NUR dafür gedacht, das Auffinden der entsprechenden Orte in Ihrer Seekarte zu erleichtern. Ungefährer Mass-stab: 25mm = 1sm.

6 Die Namen der Städte und Dörfer sind mit GROSSEN BUCHSTABEN geschrieben.

7 Jeder Kartenausschnitt zeigt einen oder mehrere Standpunkte, von denen die jeweilige Ansicht gesehen wird. Der gekennzeichnete Sektor gibt den Blickwinkel an. Mehrere nebeneinanderliegende Standortsymbole bedeuten, das die obige Ansicht eine Zusammensetzung mehrerer überlappender Bilder ist.

8 Blaue Markierungslinien auf der Seekarte bezeichnen den dargestellten Ausschnitt der Ansicht.

9 Auf manchen Seiten sind zwei übereinanderliegende Ansichten mit jeweils eigenen Erläuterungen dargestellt. Enthalten beide Ansichten dasselbe Objekt, wird dieses bei beiden Ansichten bezeichnet, und durch eine gemeinsame Linie mit der zugehörigen Position im Seekartenausschnitt verbunden. Wird die Bezeichnung des Objekts bei der unteren Ansicht *nicht* wiederholt, ist das Objekt nur in der *oberen* Ansicht sichtbar. Das zur obigen Ansicht gehörende Blickpunktsymbol ist mit 'TOP' bezeichnet.

10 Weitere Einzelheiten wie Leuchtfeuersektoren, Hafenannäherungen und vergrösserte Ansichten von Navigationsmarken sind an geeigneten Stellen der einzelnen Seiten eingefügt.

11 NORDEN is immer oben, wenn nicht anders angegeben.

Changes in coastal appearance from different viewpoints

The 'views' give accurate outlines of the coast, headlands, islands, prominent rocks etc as seen from the 'eye' positions. From closer in to the land, or from further out to sea, or from a distance to either side, their appearance will be different.
The changes take place in predictable ways, enabling you to identify the coast easily.

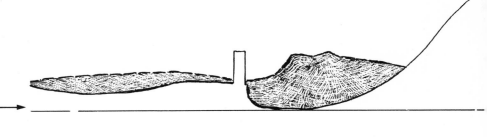

FROM CLOSER IN TO SHORE the apparent height of the nearest parts of the coast will increase. The 'lighthouse' here is increased in prominence.
NOTE THOUGH THAT THE DISTANT BACKGROUND DOES NOT CHANGE MUCH. ——————▶

THIS IS A DIAGRAM OF A TYPICAL VIEW SEEN FROM THE 'EYE'. ——————▶

FROM FURTHER OUT TO SEA the foreground is reduced in apparent height but retains its general shape.
AGAIN NOTE THAT THE DISTANT BACKGROUND IS PRACTICALLY UNCHANGED. ——————▶

When the coast is seen from further to left or right the foreground will appear to be shifted bodily the opposite way: the drawings below show the effect when the viewpoint is moved towards the middle of the page.

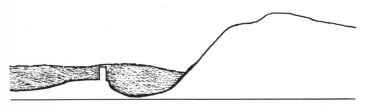

ACTUAL
VIEWPOINT

This is the effect if the actual viewpoint is to the RIGHT of the 'eye' on the chart.

This is the effect if the actual viewpoint is to the LEFT of the 'eye' on the chart.

The rule therefore is to divide the view mentally into FOREGROUND and BACKGROUND. Imagine the BACKGROUND UNCHANGED, with the FOREGROUND INCREASED IN SIZE (when nearer to shore), DECREASED IN SIZE (when further out to sea), or SHIFTED BODILY LEFT (when to the right of the eye') or RIGHT (when to the left of the eye).

Identifying coastal features

Lighthouses

A lighthouse at night is very conspicuous; by day, it may be a very different matter. Nor is the height of the light given on charts any sure guide to whether or not it will attract notice during the day. The Portland lighthouse is a tall structure standing on the low tip of Portland Bill and is visible for miles. The lighthouse of Beachy Head though, looks remarkably small at sea level, by contrast to the great cliff rising behind it. In most cases, therefore, we have given enlarged views of each building.

Churches

Many of these are marked on charts as 'conspic'. We have found, though, that a number of them are difficult to discern, being lost among trees or buildings; our views, therefore, show only those churches which can still be seen clearly. The enlarged details show their outlines, in particular the shapes of their towers, as seen from two or three miles away.

Other Buildings

Rapid changes take place along the coastline and many buildings once conspicuous are no longer so. They may be hidden behind new developments or have near neighbours which are far more noticeable. We have only indicated buildings that can be seen and reasonably easily identified.

Harbour Works

It is surprising how unobtrusive can be the appearance of even large breakwaters, quays etc when seen from seaward, especially at high water. Usually it is the buildings of the town behind the harbour that can be seen most distinctly. In our approach views we have tried to indicate the position of the harbour entrance in relation to bigger objects in the neighbourhood.

Monuments

These are popular features with chart makers and indeed many are of great service to navigation. It is necessary, though, to know their shape and relative size. Often they appear much smaller than one might expect. A structure 6m tall may be almost invisible, one 12m tall little better, and even a substantial pillar 30m high can seem quite trifling from a distance of two or three miles. Of course, to sailors familiar with the coastline, the small dark object on some distant hill may be immediately obvious and useful, but a newcomer could never identify it.

Islands

Charts show islands in plan shape and give little indication of their appearance. Our views all show the outline of islands or islets, which makes identification much easier. Nonetheless, they can frequently be totally invisible against a background of cliffs or other rocks. We have ourselves sailed 400m off an island and been completely unable to separate it from its background.

Headlands

Just as islands may resemble headlands projecting from the coastline, so headlands may resemble islands from some angles. Each one has a characteristic shape: Portland, for example, is like an island tapering seawards; St Albans Head has steep upper cliffs falling to tumbled rocks below; Selsey Bill, however, is so low lying as to be almost invisible, only a few houses and a coastguard station rising from the sea! Since headland recognition is essential to good navigation, we have usually given several aspects of each one, as approached from different directions. Note particularly that the shape of a headland when it is very close is not a certain guide to its appearance from a distance.

Caravan Sites

These, with their large numbers of light-coloured vans massed together, are very easily discernible. They are frequently visible for several miles out to sea and may create a definite pattern which is identifiable from some distance. However, it is better to use the presence of a caravan park as confirmation of a position rather than as an identification mark in itself, since they are obviously subject to change in outline and size. All those we have shown are large and would certainly be visible in normal conditions.

Radio Masts and Towers

Though these are some of the largest objects on the coast, often several hundred feet tall, they are not so conspicuous as might be expected. The masts are extremely thin openwork structures, and at a distance of some miles are not easily picked out. In lowering visibility they are the first objects to disappear. Also in places such as the Isle of Wight, there may be so many within a short distance as to make it impossible to identify any one for certain — so making all useless for navigation!

Military Installations

Certain military installations, especially radar scanners, are visible from seaward, but have had to be omitted from the views.

Glossary and Abbreviations

English	French	German	Dutch
approximate (approx)	approximatif	ungefähr	ongeveer
auxiliary (aux)	auxiliaire	Hilfs-	hulp
bearing	relèvement	Peilung	peiling
beacon (bn)	balise	Bake	baken
bell	cloche	Glocke	mistbel
black (Blk)	noir	schwarz	zwart
breakwater	brise-lames	Wellenbrecher	golfbreker
buoy (by)	bouée	Tonne	ton
can buoy	bouée cylindrique	Stumpftonne	stompe ton
castle (Cas)	château	Schloss	kasteel
channel	canal, chenal	Fahrwasser	vaarwater
church (ch)	église	Kirche	kerk
cliffs	falaises	Klippen	klip
coastguard (CG)	garde côtière	Küstenwache	kuswachtpost
conical buoy (stbd by)	bouée conique	Spitztonne	spitse ton
conspicuous (conspic)	visible, en évidence	auffällig	kenbar
diaphone (Dia)	diaphone	Pressluftsirene	diafoon
dock	dock	Dock	dok
dries	assèche	trockenfallend	droogvallend
east (E)	est	Ost	oost
entrance	entrée	Einfahrt	ingang
fixed beacon (bn)	balise fixe	feste Bake	kopbaken
fixed light (F)	feu fixe	Festfeuer (F)	vast licht (V)
flagstaff	mât	Flaggenmast	vlaggestok
flashing light (Fl)	feu à éclats	Blinkfeuer	schitterlicht
fort	fort	Fort	fort
green (G)	vert	grün	groen (gn)
group occulting light (GpOcc)	feu à occultations groupées	unterbrochenes Gruppenfeuer	groeponderbroken licht
harbour (Hr)	port, havre	Hafen	haven
head (Hd)	cap	Landspitze	voorgebergte
hill	colline	Hügel	heuvel
in line	aligné	in Linie	ineen
island(s) (Is)	île(s)	Insel(n)	eiland
jetty	jetée	Anlegesteg	pier
leading light	feu d'alignement	Richtfeuer	geleidelicht
leading line	alignement	Leitlinie	geleidelijn
least depth	profondeur minimum	Mindesttiefe	minste diepte
light buoy (LB)	bouée lumineuse	Leuchttonne	lichtboei
lighthouse (LH)	phare	Leuchtturm	lichtvuutoren
lookout	vigie	Wache	uitkijk
metre (m)	mètre	Meter	meter
monument (mont)	monument	Denkmal	monument
nautical mile (M)	mille marin	Seemeile	zeemijl
nautophone (Nauto)	nautophone	Membransender	nautofoon
north (N)	nord	Nord	noord
obscured (obsc)	masqué	verdunkelt	duister
occasional (occas)	occasionnel	gelegentlich	nu en dan
occulting light (Occ)	feu à occultations	unterbrochenes Feuer	onderbroken licht
off-lying dangers extend	dangers sétendant... au large	Gefahren, die ... vor der Küste liegen	voor de kust liggend gevaren reiken...in zee
orange (Or)	orange	orange	oranje
point (Pt)	pointe	Huk	punt
port	bâbord	Backbord	bakboord
quarry	carrière	Steinbruch	steengroeve
quick flashing light (QkFl)	feu scintillant	Funkelfeuer	flikkerlicht
radio mast (ro tr)	pylone	Funkmast	radiomast
red (R)	rouge	rot	rood
reef	récif	Riff	rif
rock (Rk)	roche	Fels	rotsgrond
seaward	vers le large	seewärts	buiten
second (time) (s)	second	Sekunde	sekonde
sector (sect)	secteur	Sektor	sector
shingle	galets	grober Kies	Keisteen
shoal	haut fond	Untiefe	ondiepte
siren	sirène	Sirene	mistsirene
south (S)	sud	Süd	zuid
starboard	tribord	Steuerbord	stuurboord
sunken rock	roche submergée	Unterwasserklippe	blinde klip
tower (tr)	tour, tourelle	Turm	toren
true (T)	vrai	rechtweisend	rechtwijzende, ware
west (W)	ouest	West	west
white (W)	blanc	weiss	wit

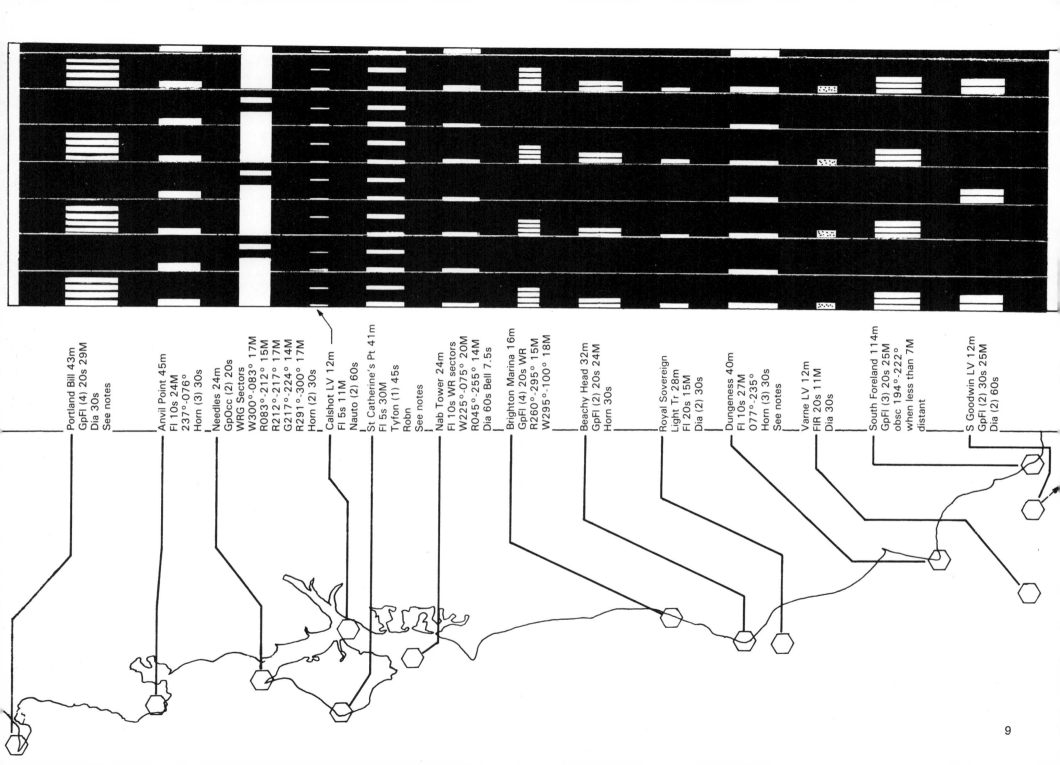

Portland Bill 43m
GpFl (4) 20s 29M
Dia 30s
See notes

Anvil Point 45m
Fl 10s 24M
237°-076°
Horn (3) 30s

Needles 24m
GpOcc (2) 20s
WRG Sectors
W300°-083° 17M
R083°-212° 15M
R212°-217° 17M
G217°-224° 14M
R291°-300° 17M
Horn (2) 30s

Calshot LV 12m
Fl 5s 11M
Nauto (2) 60s

St Catherine's Pt 41m
Fl 5s 30M
Tyfon (1) 45s
Robn
See notes

Nab Tower 24m
Fl 10s WR sectors
W225°-075° 20M
R045°-255° 14M
Dia 60s Bell 7.5s

Brighton Marina 16m
GpFl (4) 20s WR
R260°-295° 15M
W295°-100° 18M

Beachy Head 32m
GpFl (2) 20s 24M
Horn 30s

Royal Sovereign
Light Tr 28m
Fl 20s 15M
Dia (2) 30s

Dungeness 40m
Fl 10s 27M
077°-235°
Horn (3) 30s
See notes

Varne LV 12m
FlR 20s 11M
Dia 30s

South Foreland 114m
GpFl (3) 20s 25M
obsc 194°-222°
when less than 7M
distant

S Goodwin LV 12m
GpFl (2) 30s 25M
Dia (2) 60s

9

Portland Bill from westward

DANGER — RACE: An extensive and dangerous race develops SE of Portland Bill with the east-going tide and SW of the Bill on the west-going tide: check tidal atlases

Portland Bill LH 43m
GpFl (4) 20s 29M and FR
See note page 11

Portland Bill from southward

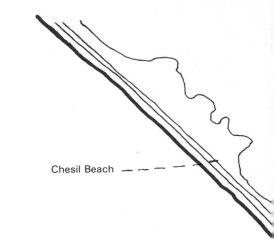

Chesil Beach — — —

Portland Bill from eastward

To PORTLAND and WEYMOUTH

ROUNDING THE PORTLAND PENINSULA: Owing to the Portland Race it is safest to pass the Bill 3-7M to seaward, clear of the race position as shown on charts. An inside passage exists in nearly all conditions, less than ½M from the shore of the Bill. There is almost always a strong south-going stream both E and W of the peninsula which can carry an underpowered boat into the race area.

Generally speaking, the Bill is best rounded at low water.

Local advice from the coastguards should be obtained: constant watch is maintained on the Bill and the regional centre is at Wyke Regis

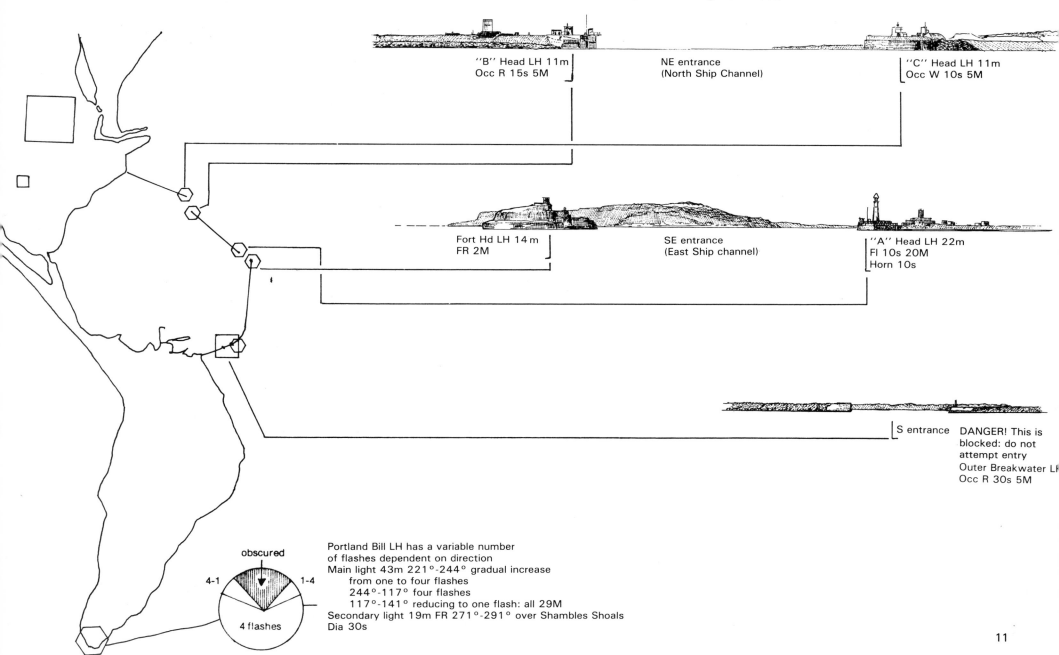

PORTLAND HARBOUR
(Yacht anchorage to NW side)

"B" Head LH 11m
Occ R 15s 5M

NE entrance
(North Ship Channel)

"C" Head LH 11m
Occ W 10s 5M

Fort Hd LH 14m
FR 2M

SE entrance
(East Ship channel)

"A" Head LH 22m
Fl 10s 20M
Horn 10s

S entrance   DANGER! This is
blocked: do not
attempt entry
Outer Breakwater LH
Occ R 30s 5M

obscured

4-1   1-4

4 flashes

Portland Bill LH has a variable number
of flashes dependent on direction
Main light 43m 221°-244° gradual increase
    from one to four flashes
    244°-117° four flashes
    117°-141° reducing to one flash: all 29M
Secondary light 19m FR 271°-291° over Shambles Shoals
Dia 30s

11

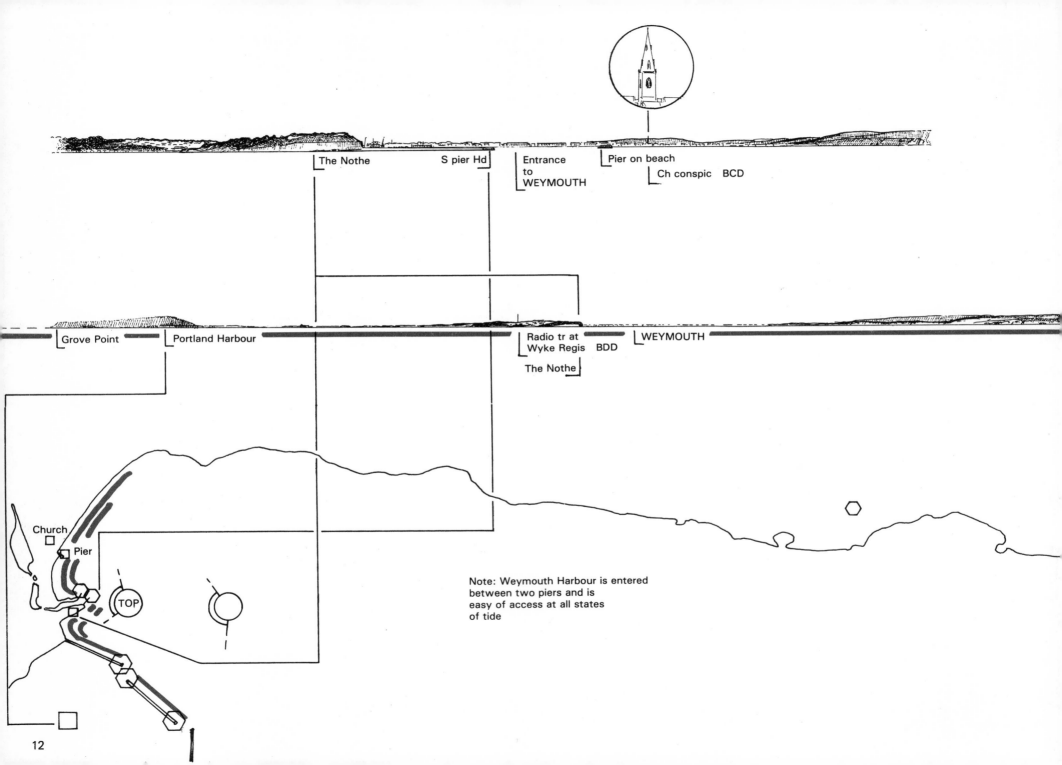

The Nothe   S pier Hd

Entrance
to
WEYMOUTH

Pier on beach

Ch conspic BCD

Grove Point   Portland Harbour

Radio tr at
Wyke Regis BDD

WEYMOUTH

The Nothe

Church

Pier

TOP

Note: Weymouth Harbour is entered
between two piers and is
easy of access at all states
of tide

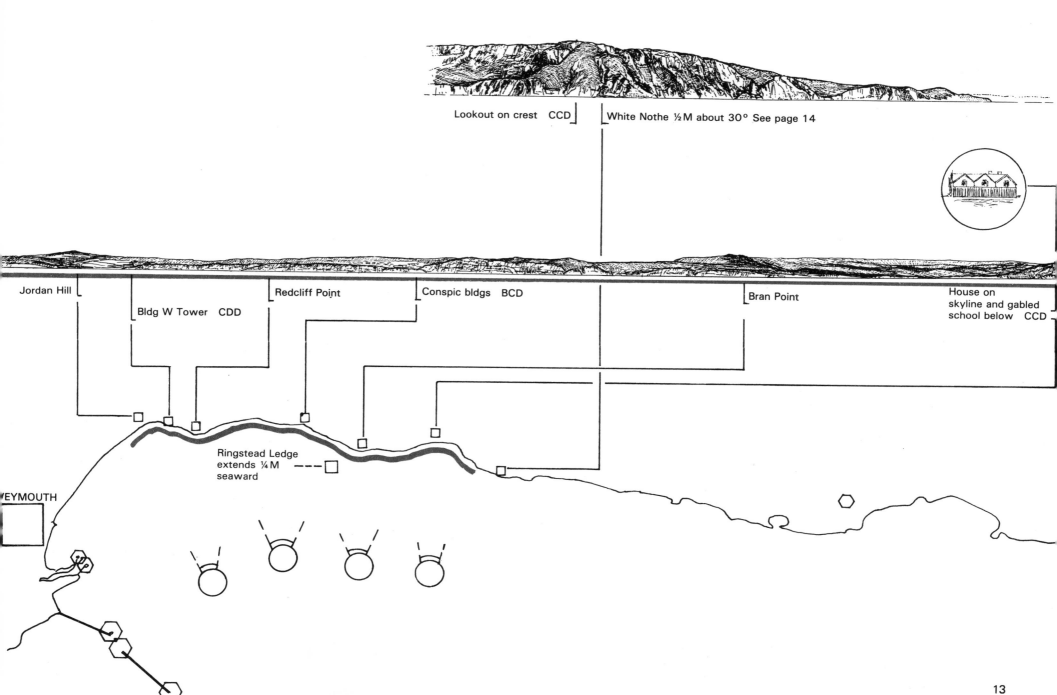

Lookout on crest   CCD

White Nothe ½M about 30° See page 14

Jordan Hill

Bldg W Tower   CDD

Redcliff Point

Conspic bldgs   BCD

Bran Point

House on skyline and gabled school below   CCD

Ringstead Ledge extends ¼M seaward

WEYMOUTH

House in trees

Lulworth Cove entrance.
Note that this is often
difficult to pick out:
Mupe Rocks W of Worbarrow
Bay are 1M E of Lulworth

WARNING: Lulworth Cove: Though this is
easy to enter, just passing E of centre
of the entrance, leave *immediately*
if an increasing wind shifts S or SW.
Swell enters the cove and exit may
become impossible

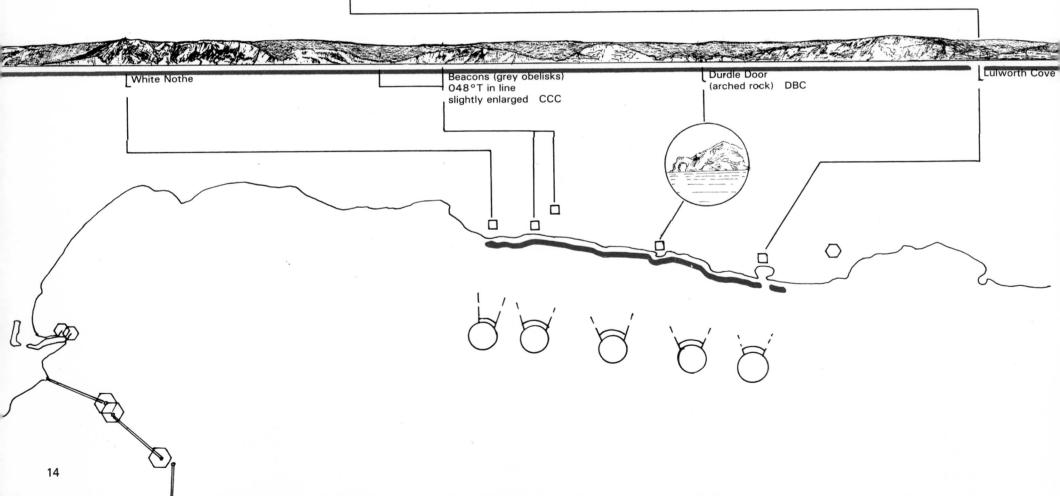

White Nothe

Beacons (grey obelisks)
048°T in line
slightly enlarged   CCC

Durdle Door
(arched rock)   DBC

Lulworth Cove

Worbarrow Tout
50° 1M

St Albans Hd
100° 2M ABB

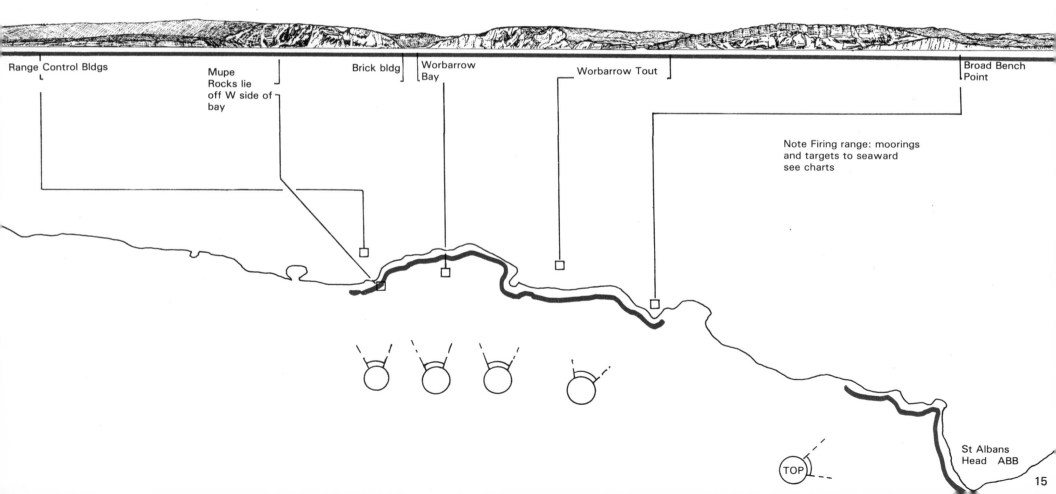

Range Control Bldgs

Mupe
Rocks lie
off W side of
bay

Brick bldg

Worbarrow
Bay

Worbarrow Tout

Broad Bench
Point

Note Firing range: moorings
and targets to seaward
see charts

TOP

St Albans
Head ABB

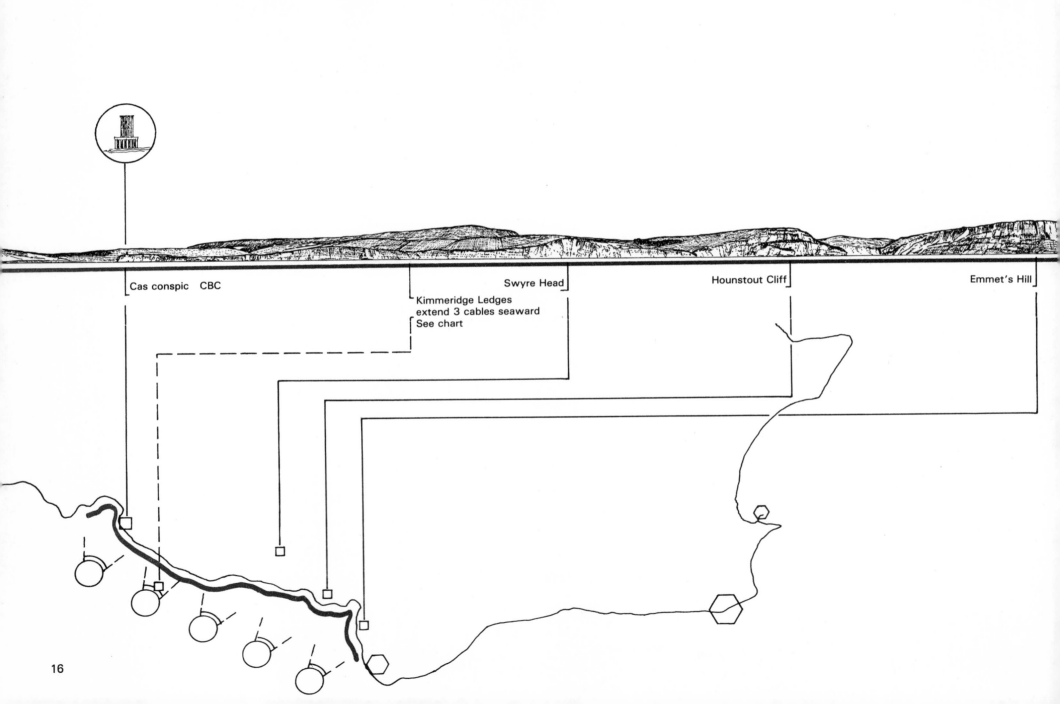

Cas conspic CBC

Swyre Head

Kimmeridge Ledges
extend 3 cables seaward
See chart

Hounstout Cliff

Emmet's Hill

16

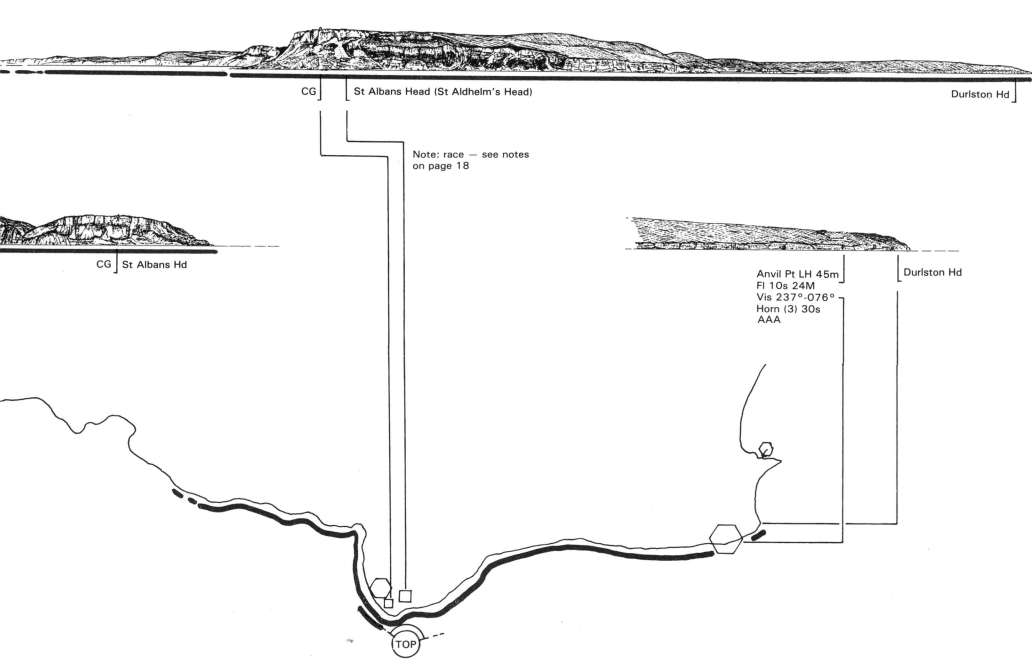

CG | St Albans Head (St Aldhelm's Head)

Durlston Hd

Note: race — see notes on page 18

CG | St Albans Hd

Anvil Pt LH 45m
Fl 10s 24M
Vis 237°-076°
Horn (3) 30s
AAA

Durlston Hd

TOP

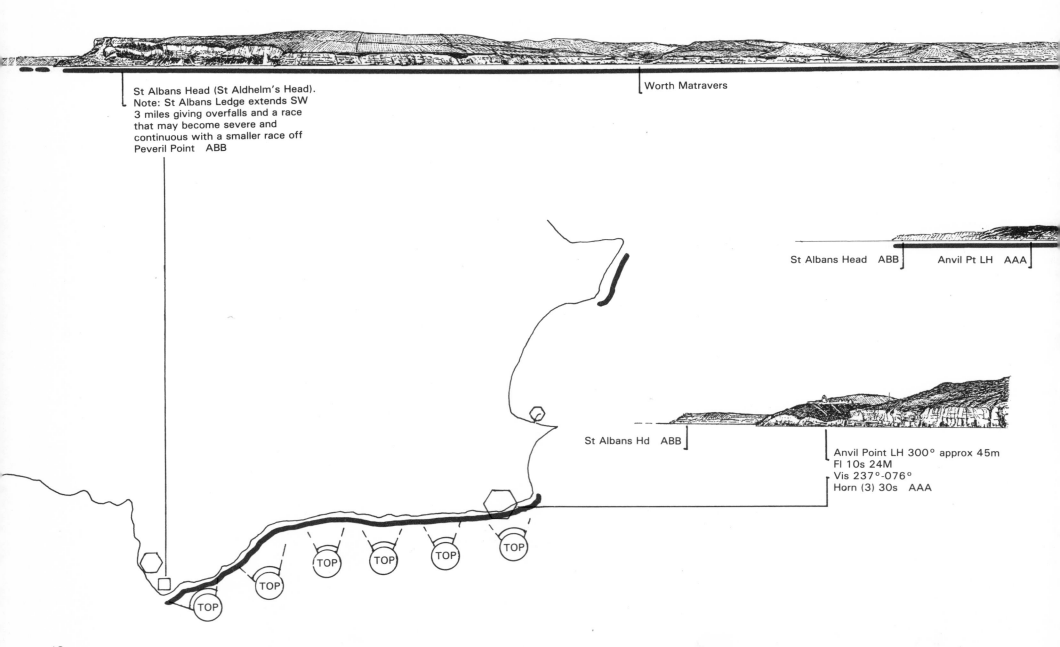

St Albans Head (St Aldhelm's Head).
Note: St Albans Ledge extends SW
3 miles giving overfalls and a race
that may become severe and
continuous with a smaller race off
Peveril Point   ABB

Worth Matravers

St Albans Head   ABB   Anvil Pt LH   AAA

St Albans Hd   ABB

Anvil Point LH 300° approx 45m
Fl 10s 24M
Vis 237°-076°
Horn (3) 30s   AAA

TOP

TOP

TOP

TOP

TOP

TOP

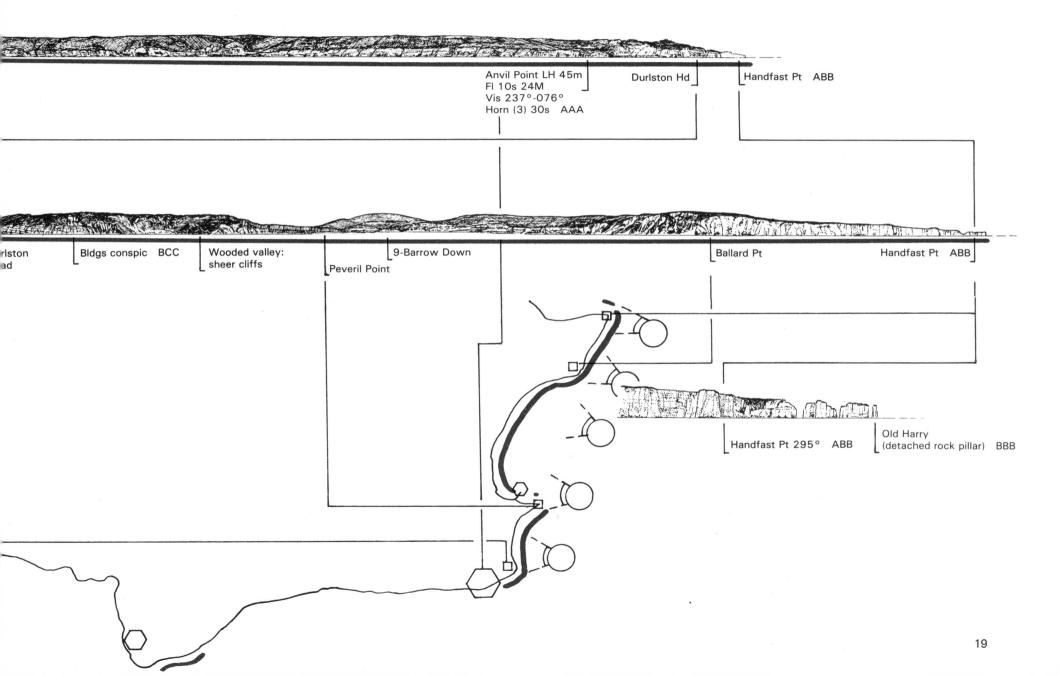

Anvil Point LH 45m
Fl 10s 24M
Vis 237°-076°
Horn (3) 30s AAA

Durlston Hd

Handfast Pt ABB

rlston
ad

Bldgs conspic BCC

Wooded valley:
sheer cliffs

Peveril Point

9-Barrow Down

Ballard Pt

Handfast Pt ABB

Handfast Pt 295° ABB

Old Harry
(detached rock pillar) BBB

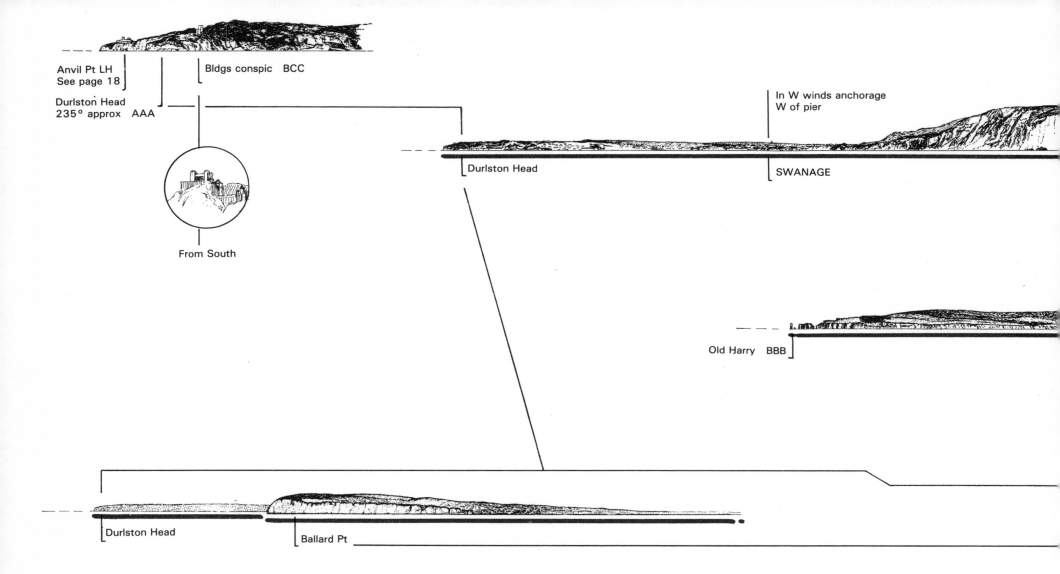

Anvil Pt LH
See page 18

Bldgs conspic   BCC

Durlston Head
235° approx   AAA

From South

In W winds anchorage
W of pier

Durlston Head

SWANAGE

Old Harry   BBB

Durlston Head

Ballard Pt

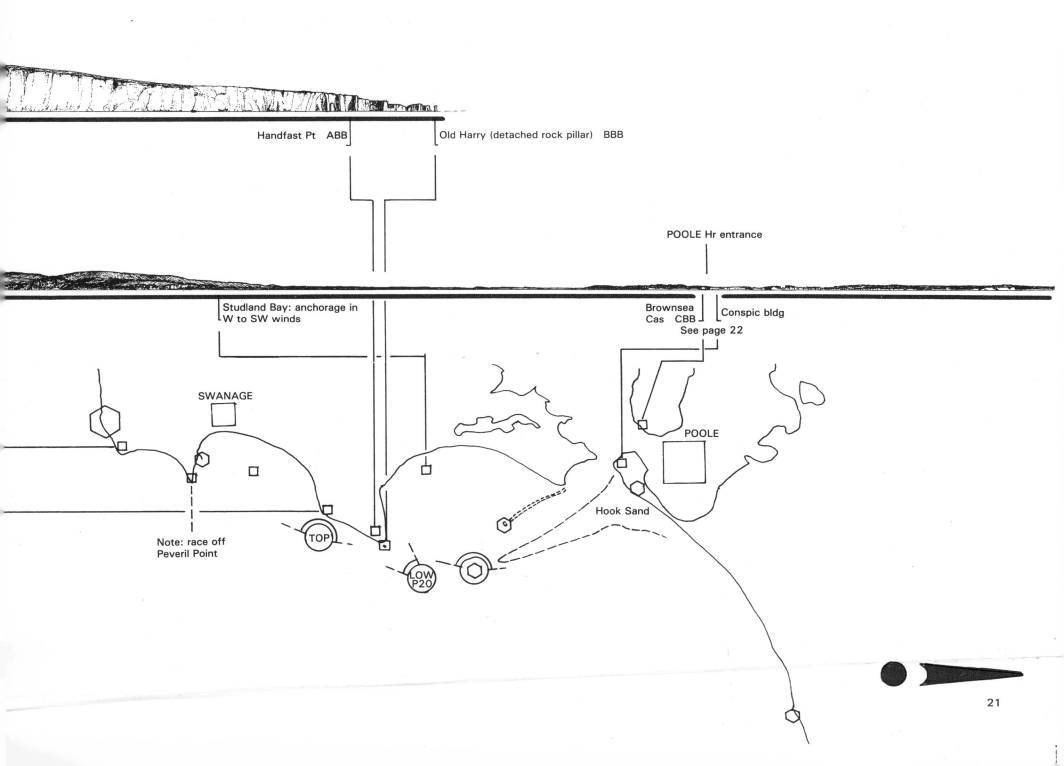

Handfast Pt   ABB   Old Harry (detached rock pillar)   BBB

POOLE Hr entrance

Studland Bay: anchorage in
W to SW winds

Brownsea
Cas   CBB   Conspic bldg
See page 22

SWANAGE

POOLE

Note: race off
Peveril Point

TOP

LOW
P20

Hook Sand

21

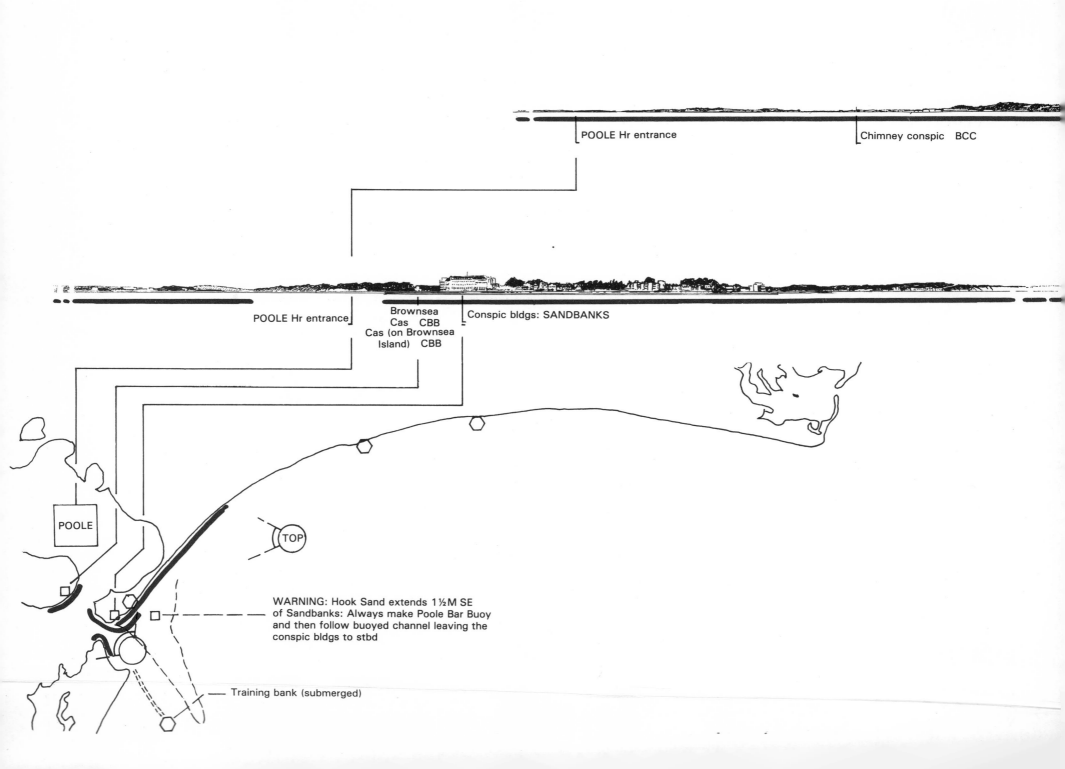

POOLE Hr entrance

Chimney conspic BCC

POOLE Hr entrance

Brownsea
Cas   CBB
Cas (on Brownsea
Island)   CBB

Conspic bldgs: SANDBANKS

POOLE

TOP

WARNING: Hook Sand extends 1½M SE
of Sandbanks: Always make Poole Bar Buoy
and then follow buoyed channel leaving the
conspic bldgs to stbd

Training bank (submerged)

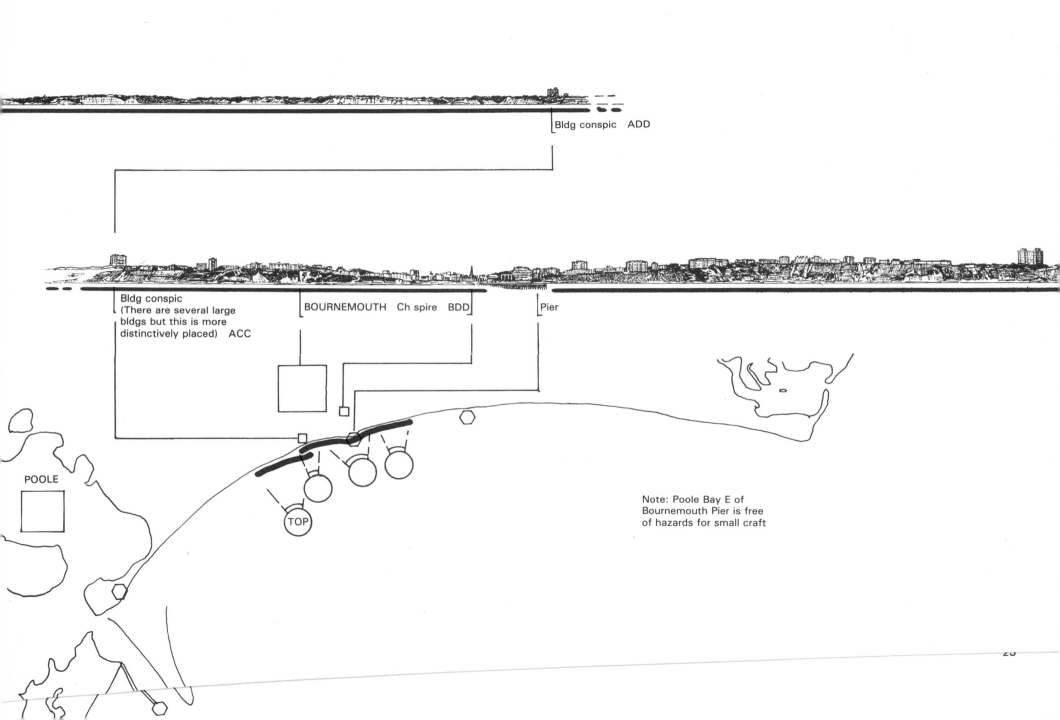

Bldg conspic   ADD

Bldg conspic
(There are several large
bldgs but this is more
distinctively placed)   ACC

BOURNEMOUTH   Ch spire   BDD

Pier

POOLE

TOP

Note: Poole Bay E of
Bournemouth Pier is free
of hazards for small craft

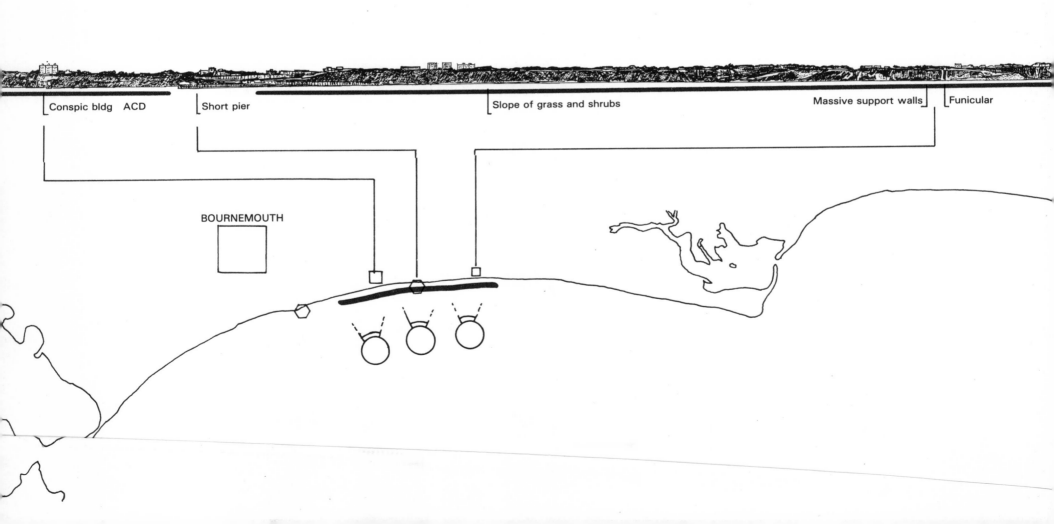

Conspic bldg ACD   Short pier   Slope of grass and shrubs   Massive support walls   Funicular

BOURNEMOUTH

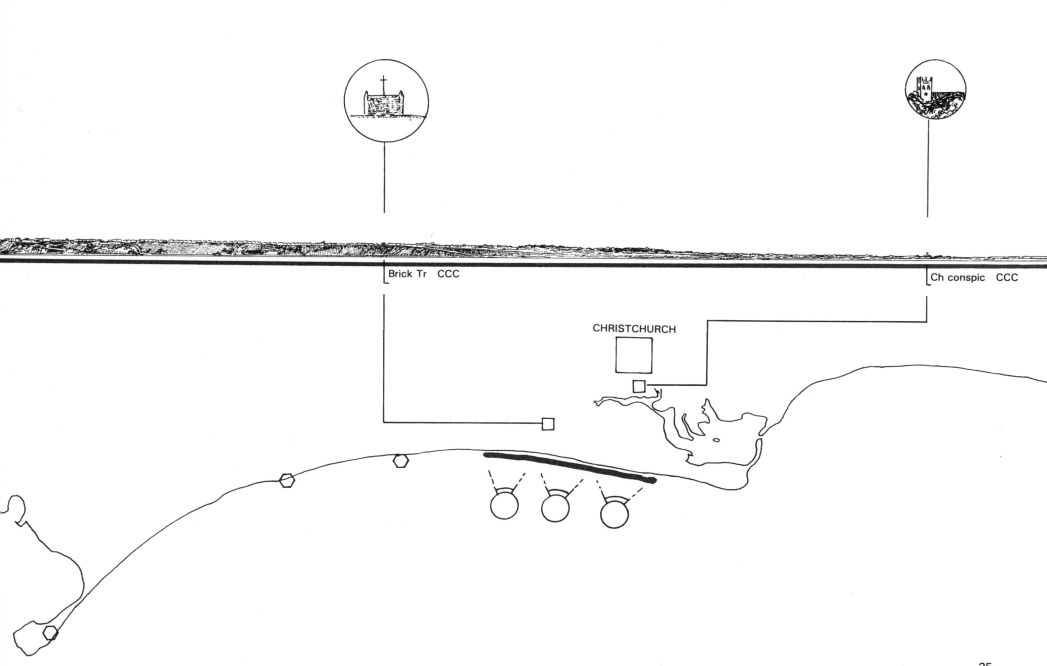

Brick Tr   CCC

Ch conspic   CCC

CHRISTCHURCH

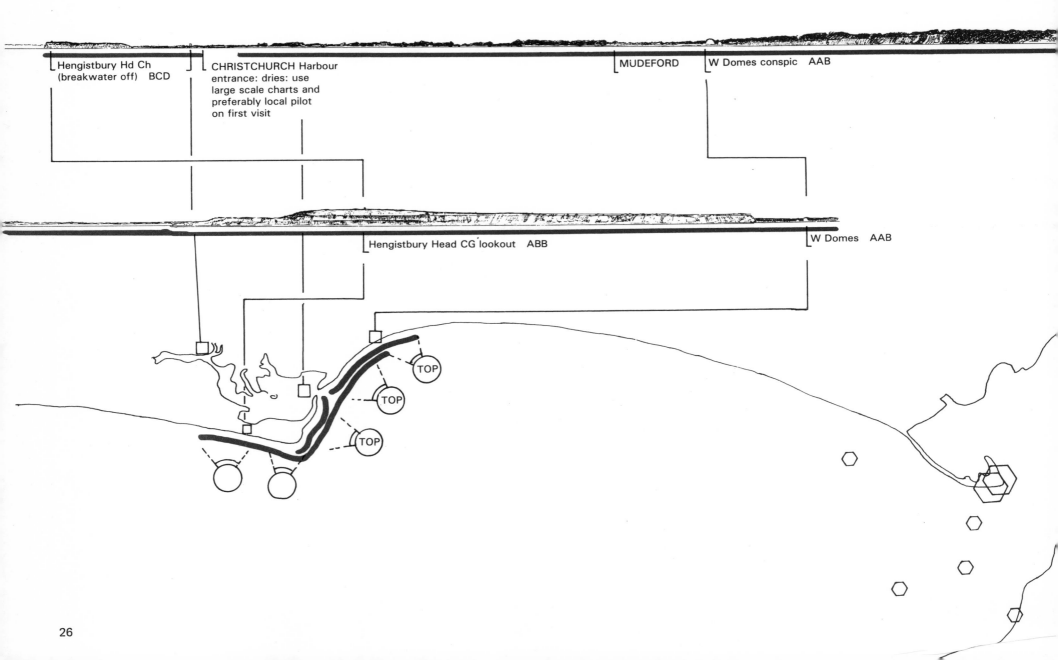

Hengistbury Hd Ch
(breakwater off) BCD

CHRISTCHURCH Harbour
entrance: dries: use
large scale charts and
preferably local pilot
on first visit

MUDEFORD

W Domes conspic   AAB

Hengistbury Head CG lookout   ABB

W Domes   AAB

TOP

TOP

TOP

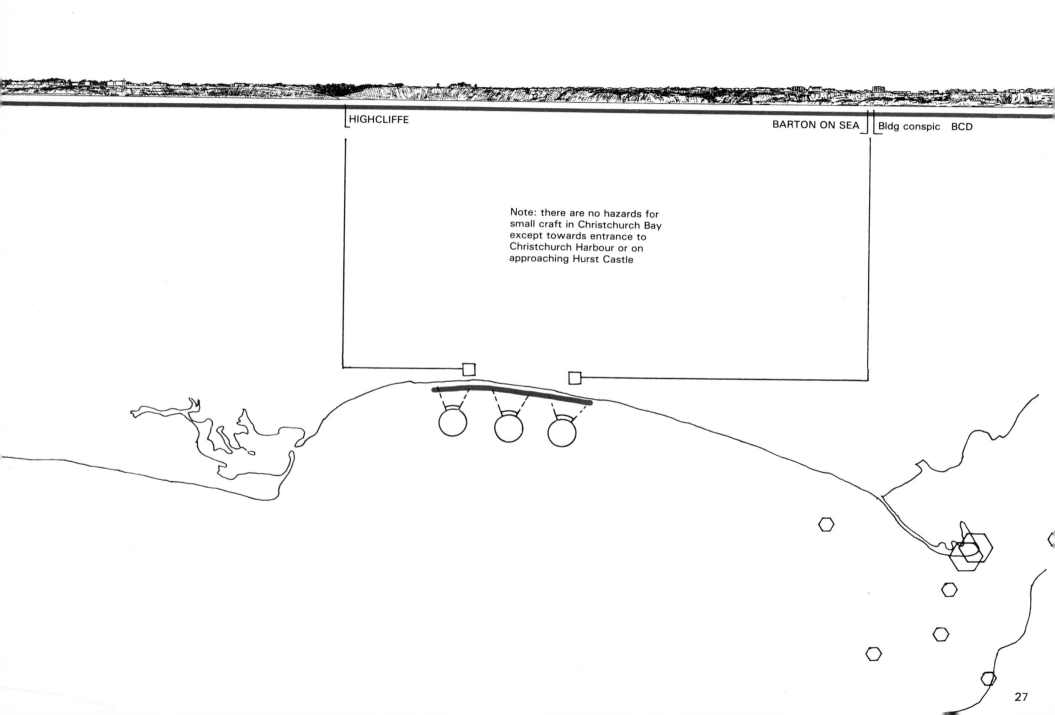

HIGHCLIFFE

BARTON ON SEA | Bldg conspic BCD

Note: there are no hazards for
small craft in Christchurch Bay
except towards entrance to
Christchurch Harbour or on
approaching Hurst Castle

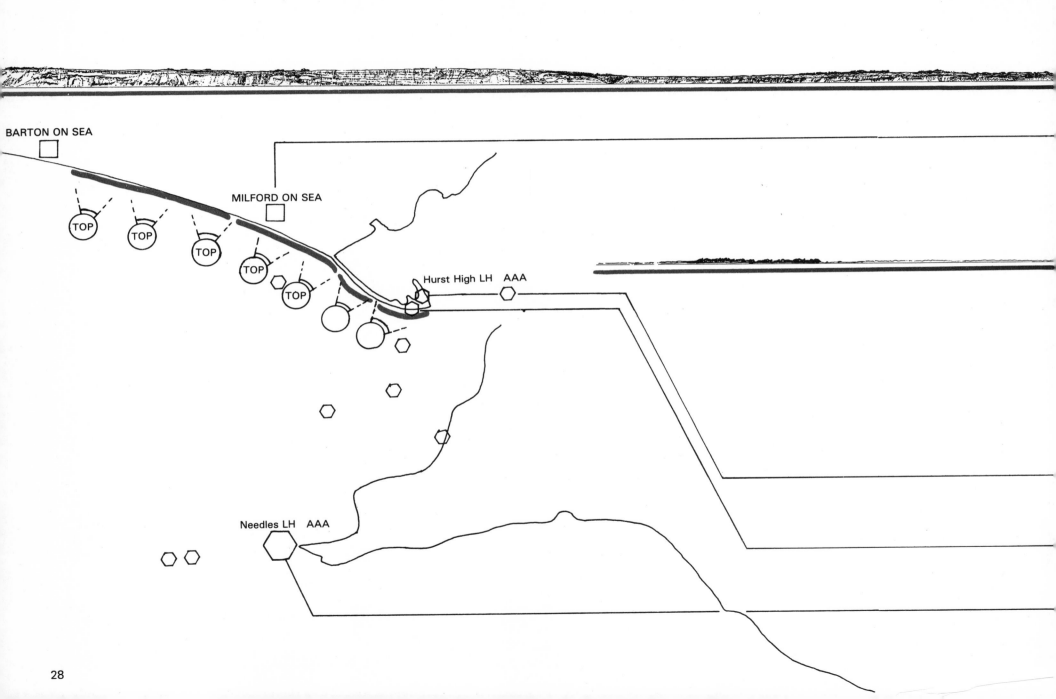

BARTON ON SEA

MILFORD ON SEA

TOP

TOP

TOP

TOP

TOP

Hurst High LH   AAA

Needles LH   AAA

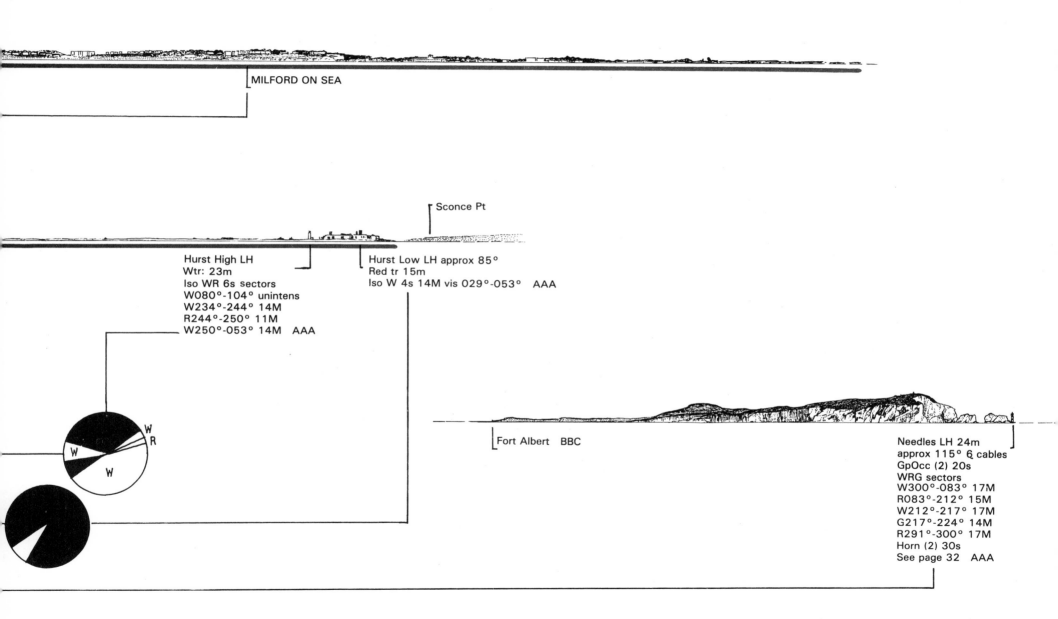

MILFORD ON SEA

Sconce Pt

Hurst High LH
Wtr: 23m
Iso WR 6s sectors
W080°-104° unintens
W234°-244° 14M
R244°-250° 11M
W250°-053° 14M   AAA

Hurst Low LH approx 85°
Red tr 15m
Iso W 4s 14M vis 029°-053°   AAA

Fort Albert   BBC

Needles LH 24m
approx 115° 6 cables
GpOcc (2) 20s
WRG sectors
W300°-083° 17M
R083°-212° 15M
W212°-217° 17M
G217°-224° 14M
R291°-300° 17M
Horn (2) 30s
See page 32   AAA

29

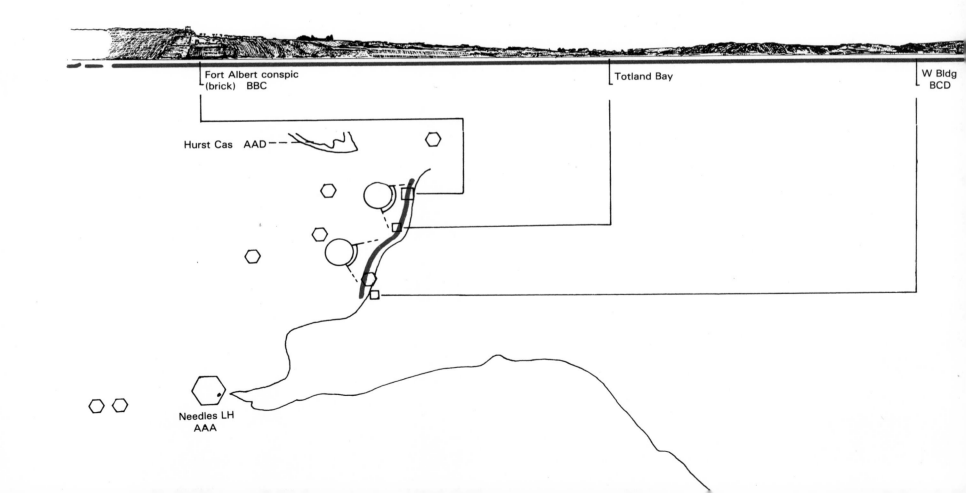

Fort Albert conspic
(brick) BBC

Totland Bay

W Bldg
BCD

Hurst Cas AAD

Needles LH
AAA

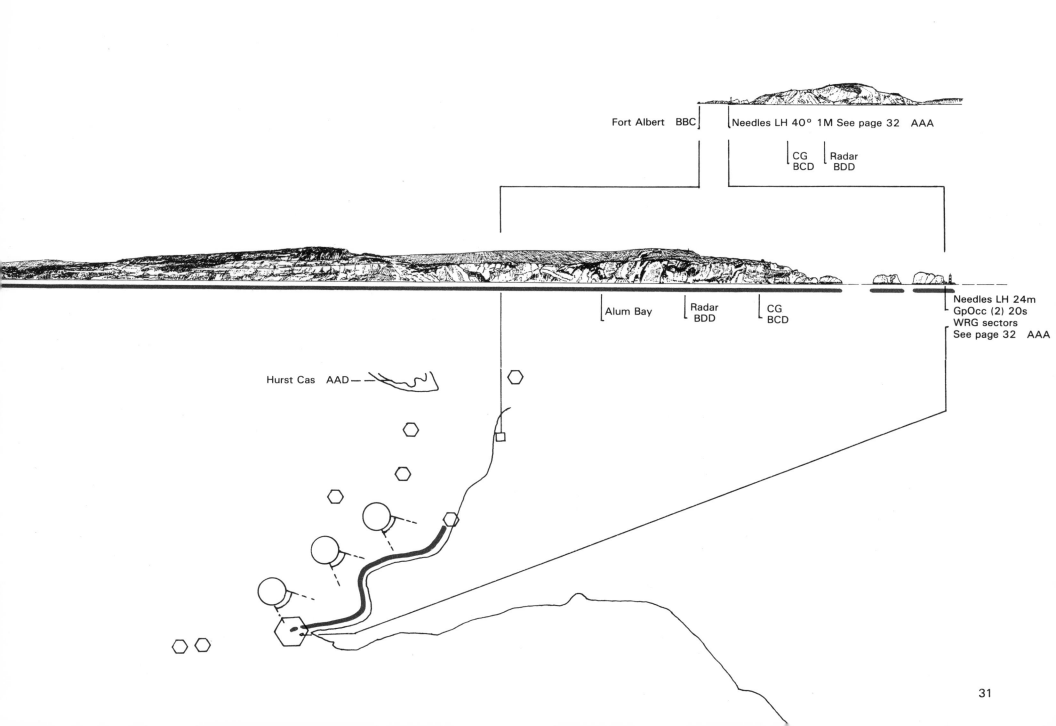

Fort Albert BBC

Needles LH 40° 1M See page 32 AAA

CG
BCD

Radar
BDD

Alum Bay

Radar
BDD

CG
BCD

Needles LH 24m
GpOcc (2) 20s
WRG sectors
See page 32 AAA

Hurst Cas AAD

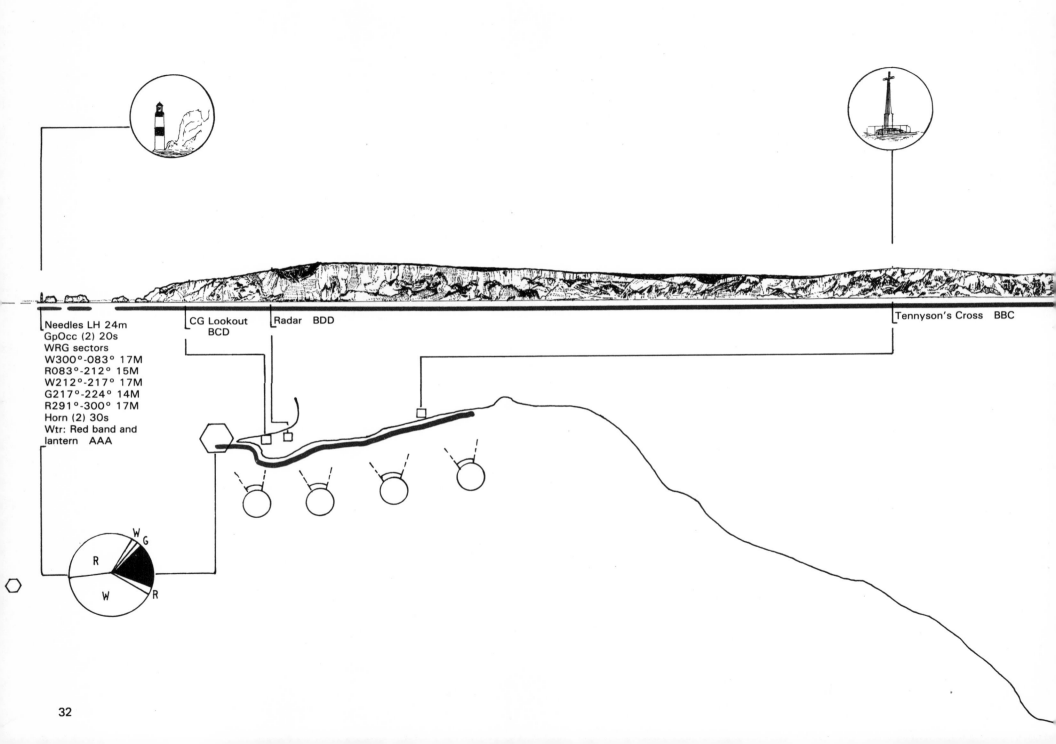

Needles LH 24m
GpOcc (2) 20s
WRG sectors
W300°-083° 17M
R083°-212° 15M
W212°-217° 17M
G217°-224° 14M
R291°-300° 17M
Horn (2) 30s
Wtr: Red band and
lantern   AAA

CG Lookout
BCD

Radar   BDD

Tennyson's Cross   BBC

W G
R
W   R

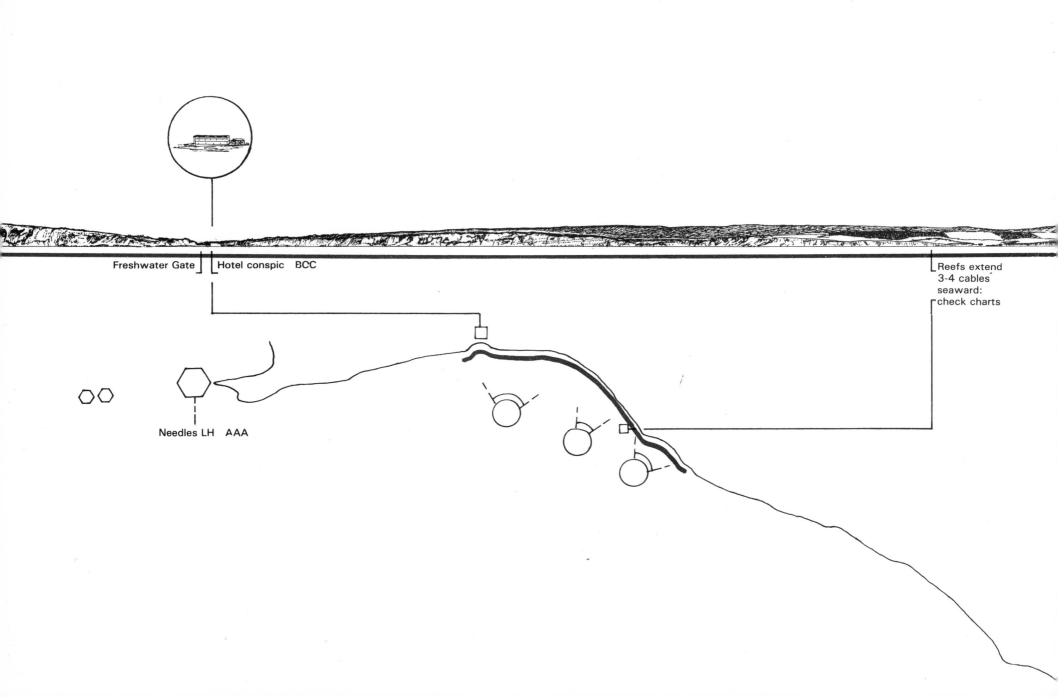

Freshwater Gate | Hotel conspic BCC

Reefs extend
3-4 cables
seaward:
check charts

Needles LH AAA

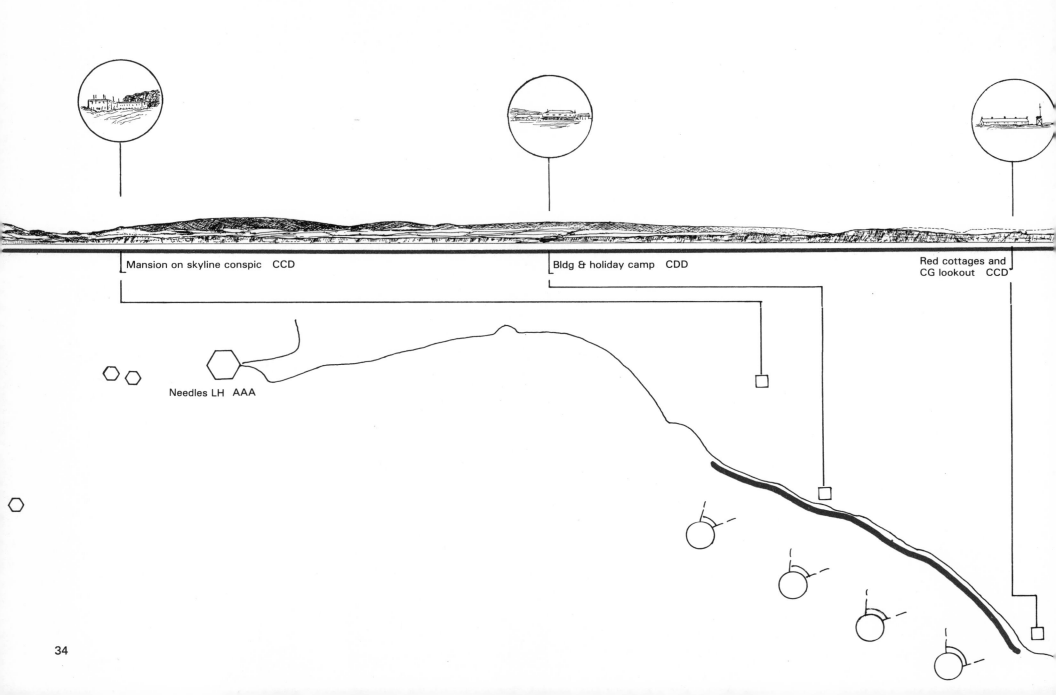

Mansion on skyline conspic   CCD

Bldg & holiday camp   CDD

Red cottages and
CG lookout   CCD

Needles LH   AAA

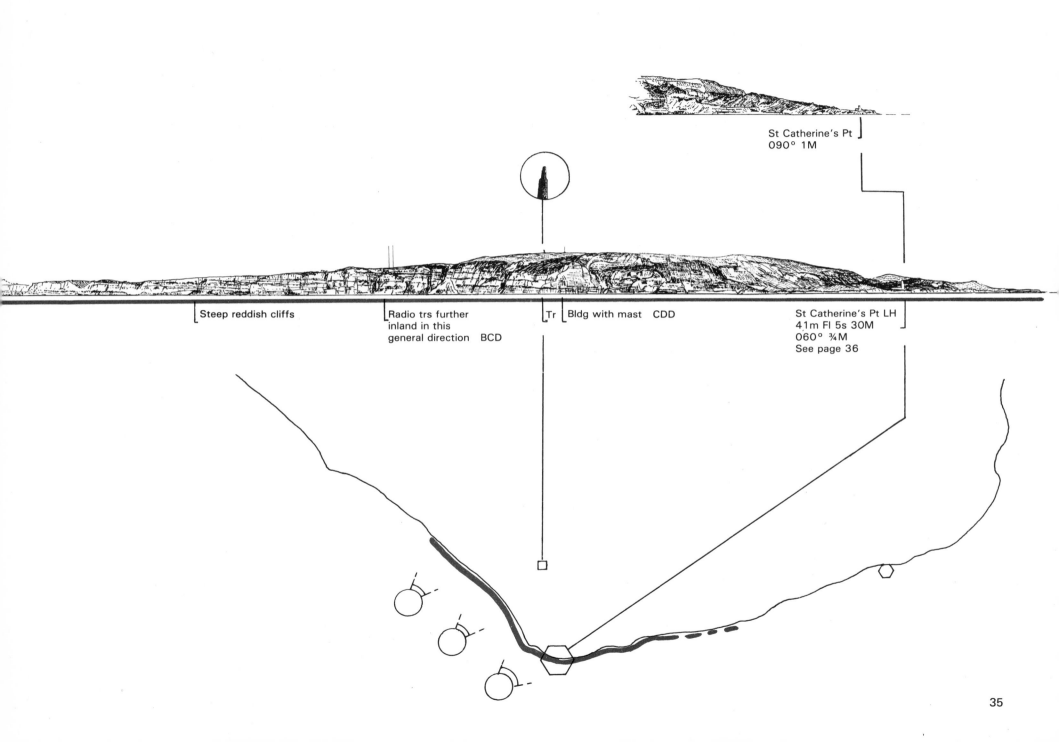

St Catherine's Pt
090° 1M

Steep reddish cliffs

Radio trs further
inland in this
general direction   BCD

Tr | Bldg with mast   CDD

St Catherine's Pt LH
41m Fl 5s 30M
060° ¾M
See page 36

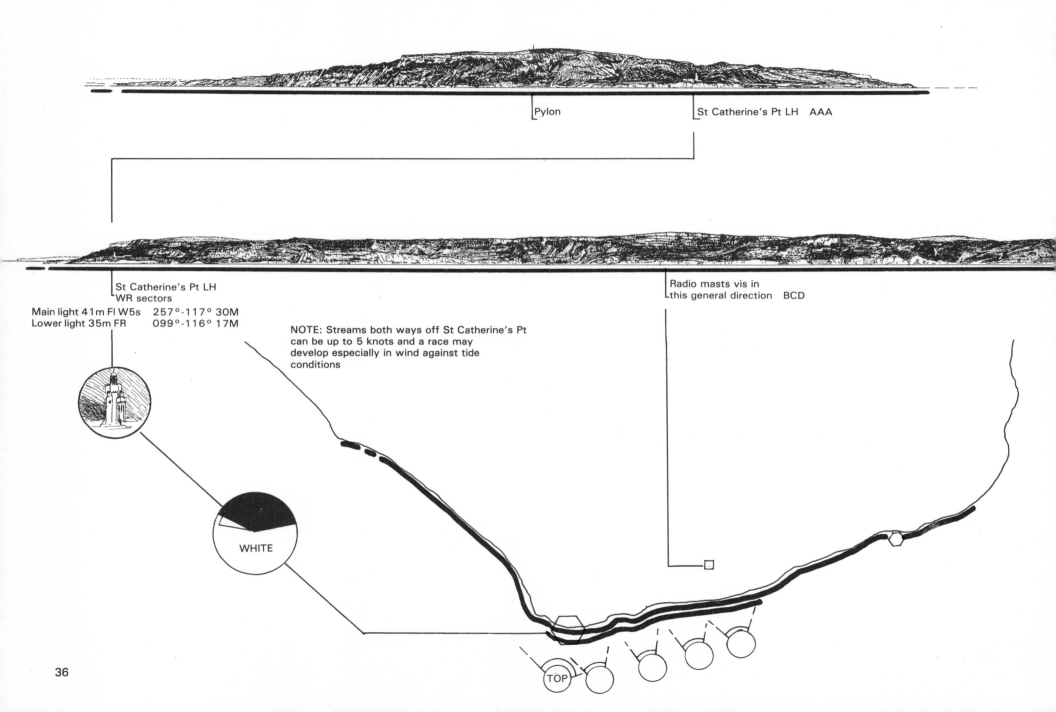

Pylon

St Catherine's Pt LH   AAA

St Catherine's Pt LH
WR sectors

Main light 41m Fl W5s   257°-117° 30M
Lower light 35m FR   099°-116° 17M

NOTE: Streams both ways off St Catherine's Pt
can be up to 5 knots and a race may
develop especially in wind against tide
conditions

Radio masts vis in
this general direction   BCD

WHITE

TOP

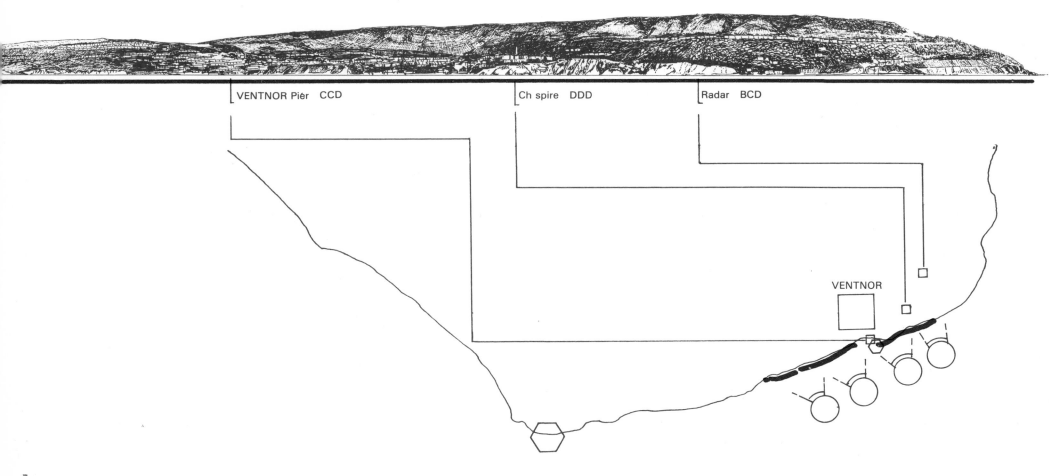

VENTNOR Piér CCD

Ch spire DDD

Radar BCD

VENTNOR

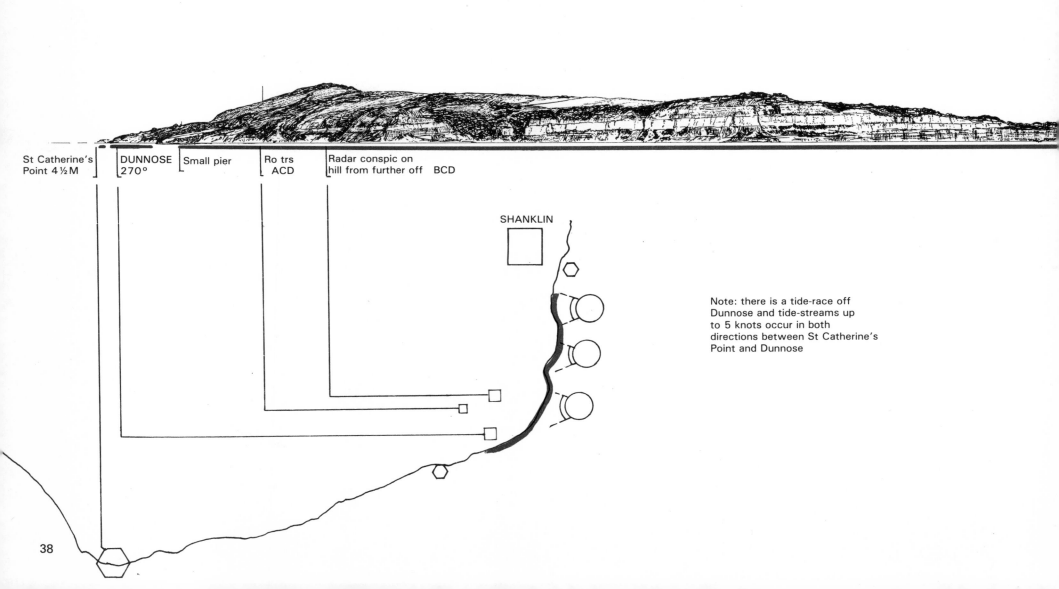

St Catherine's
Point 4½ M

DUNNOSE
270°

Small pier

Ro trs
ACD

Radar conspic on
hill from further off   BCD

SHANKLIN

Note: there is a tide-race off
Dunnose and tide-streams up
to 5 knots occur in both
directions between St Catherine's
Point and Dunnose

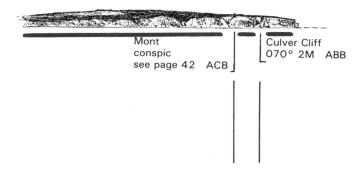

Mont
conspic
see page 42   ACB

Culver Cliff
070° 2M   ABB

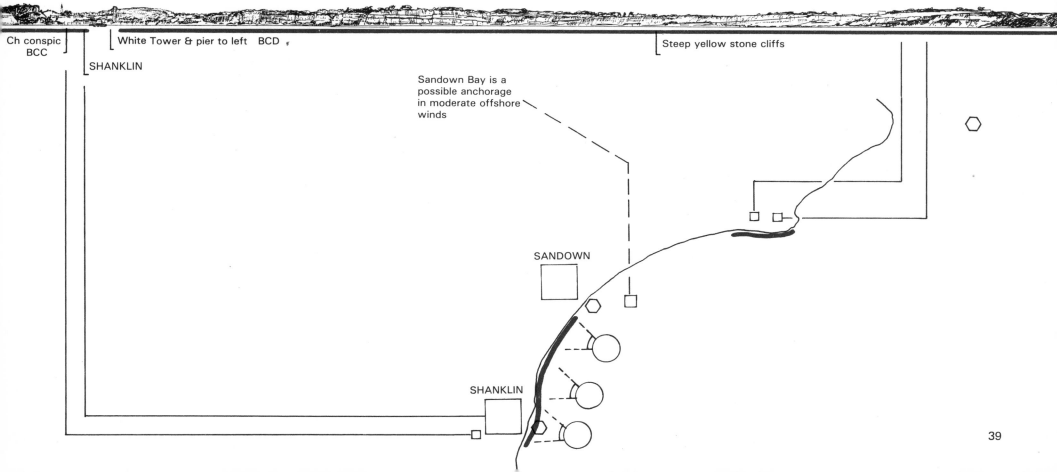

Ch conspic
BCC

White Tower & pier to left   BCD

Steep yellow stone cliffs

SHANKLIN

Sandown Bay is a
possible anchorage
in moderate offshore
winds

SANDOWN

SHANKLIN

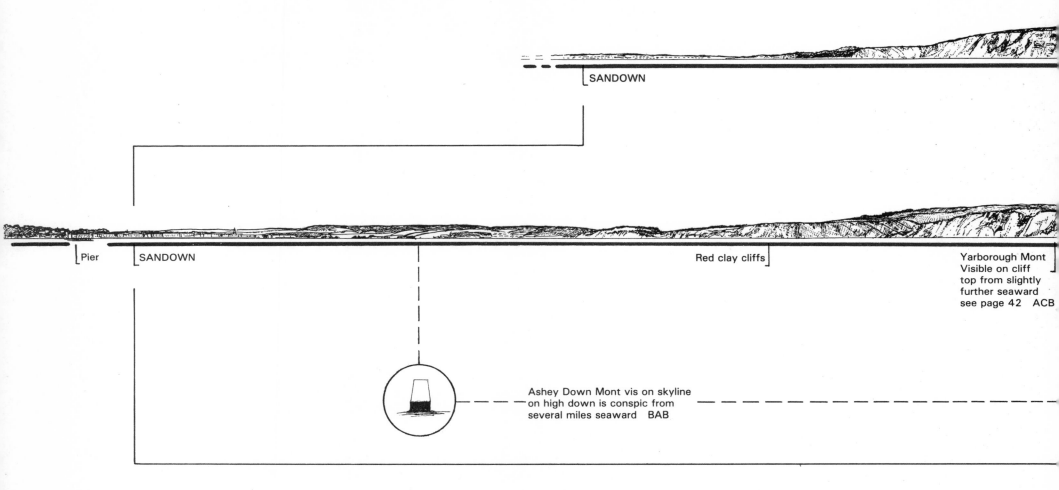

SANDOWN

Pier   SANDOWN

Red clay cliffs

Yarborough Mont
Visible on cliff
top from slightly
further seaward
see page 42   ACB

Ashey Down Mont vis on skyline
on high down is conspic from
several miles seaward   BAB

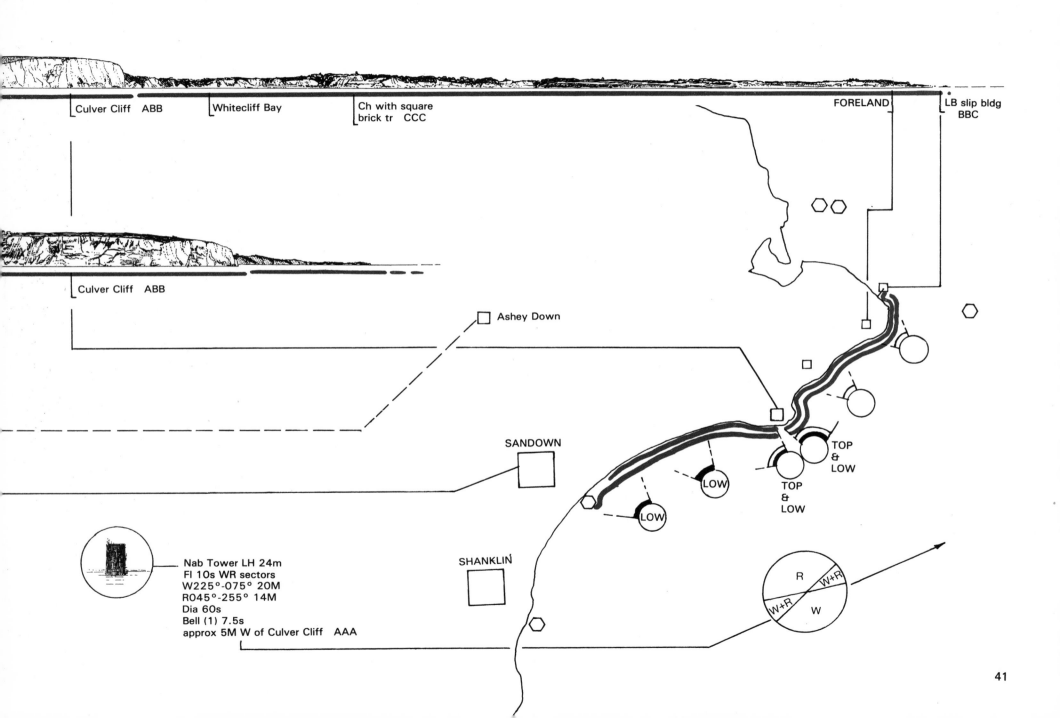

Culver Cliff ABB

Whitecliff Bay

Ch with square
brick tr CCC

FORELAND

LB slip bldg
BBC

Culver Cliff ABB

Ashey Down

SANDOWN

TOP
&
LOW

TOP
&
LOW

LOW

LOW

LOW

SHANKLIN

Nab Tower LH 24m
Fl 10s WR sectors
W225°-075° 20M
R045°-255° 14M
Dia 60s
Bell (1) 7.5s
approx 5M W of Culver Cliff AAA

R

W+R

W+R

W

41

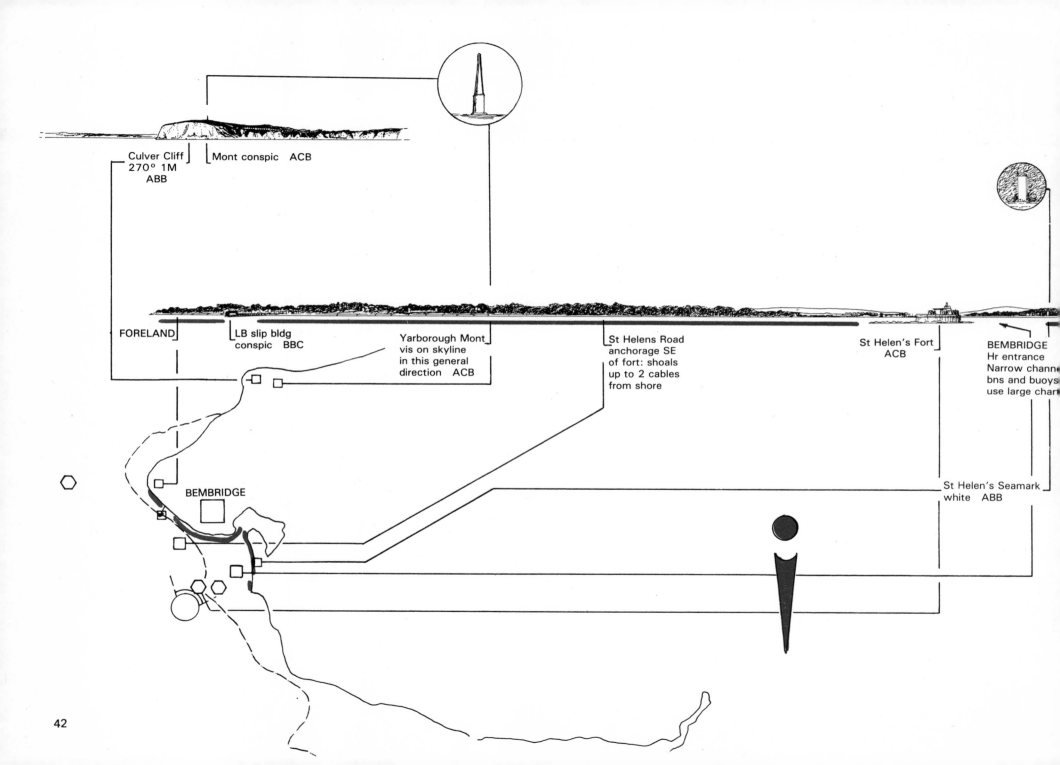

Culver Cliff
270° 1M
ABB

Mont conspic   ACB

FORELAND

LB slip bldg
conspic   BBC

Yarborough Mont
vis on skyline
in this general
direction   ACB

St Helens Road
anchorage SE
of fort: shoals
up to 2 cables
from shore

St Helen's Fort
ACB

BEMBRIDGE
Hr entrance
Narrow channe
bns and buoys
use large chart

BEMBRIDGE

St Helen's Seamark
white   ABB

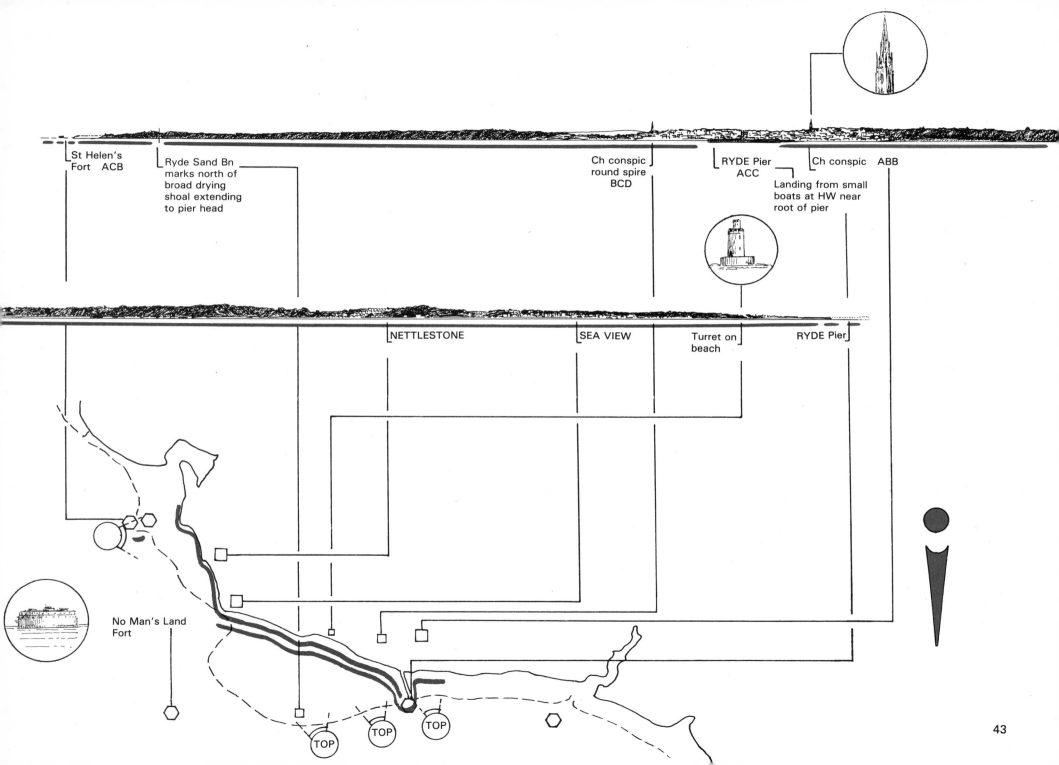

St Helen's Fort ACB

Ryde Sand Bn marks north of broad drying shoal extending to pier head

Ch conspic round spire BCD

RYDE Pier ACC

Ch conspic ABB

Landing from small boats at HW near root of pier

NETTLESTONE

SEA VIEW

Turret on beach

RYDE Pier

No Man's Land Fort

TOP

TOP

TOP

43

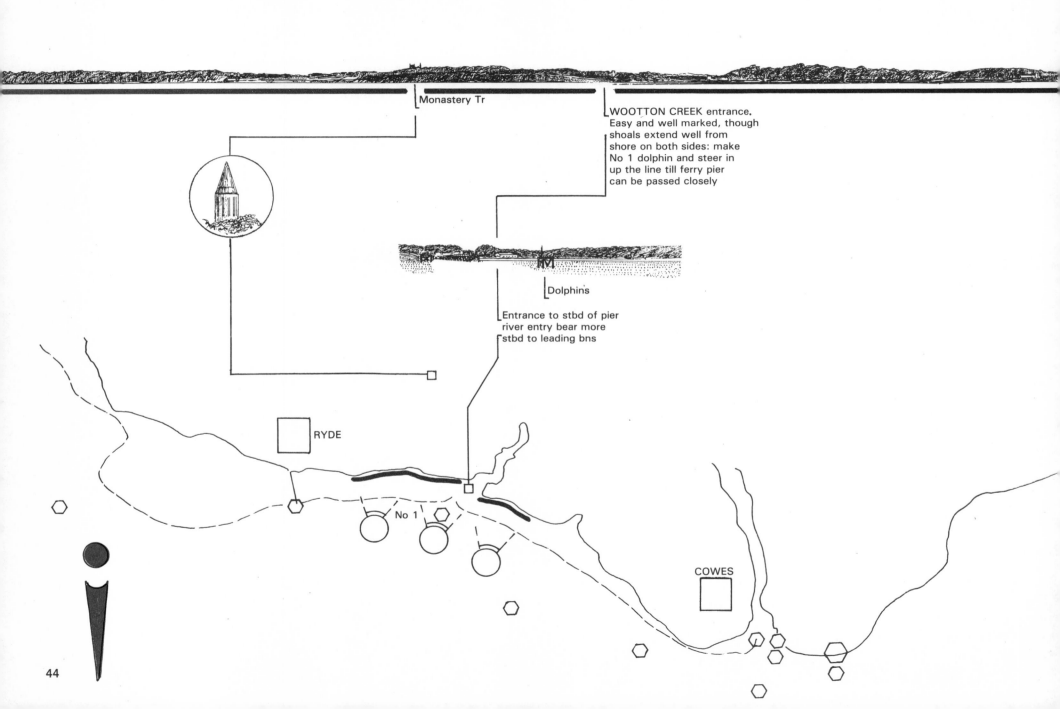

Monastery Tr

WOOTTON CREEK entrance.
Easy and well marked, though
shoals extend well from
shore on both sides: make
No 1 dolphin and steer in
up the line till ferry pier
can be passed closely

Dolphins

Entrance to stbd of pier
river entry bear more
stbd to leading bns

RYDE

No 1

COWES

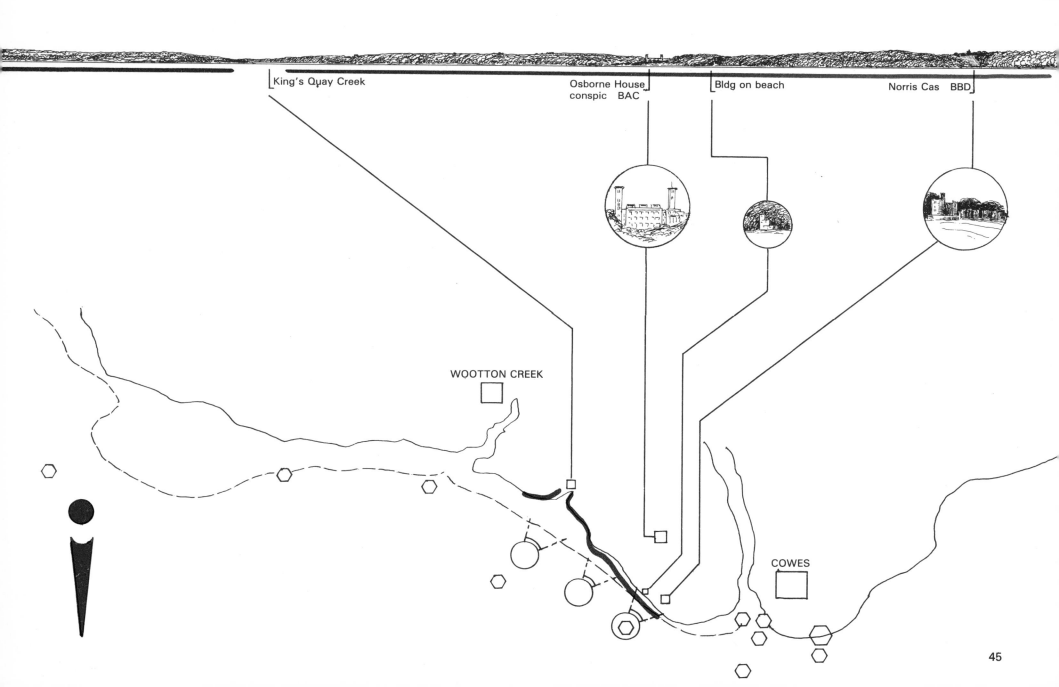

King's Quay Creek

Osborne House
conspic BAC

Bldg on beach

Norris Cas BBD

WOOTTON CREEK

COWES

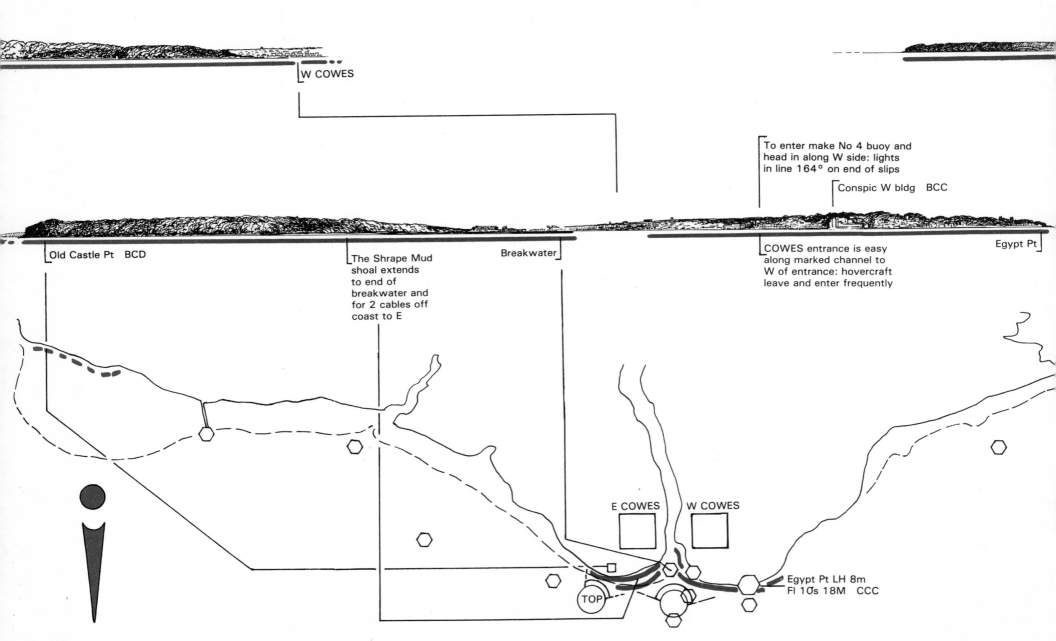

W COWES

To enter make No 4 buoy and
head in along W side: lights
in line 164° on end of slips

Conspic W bldg   BCC

Old Castle Pt   BCD

The Shrape Mud
shoal extends
to end of
breakwater and
for 2 cables off
coast to E

Breakwater

COWES entrance is easy
along marked channel to
W of entrance: hovercraft
leave and enter frequently

Egypt Pt

E COWES   W COWES

TOP

Egypt Pt LH 8m
Fl 10s 18M   CCC

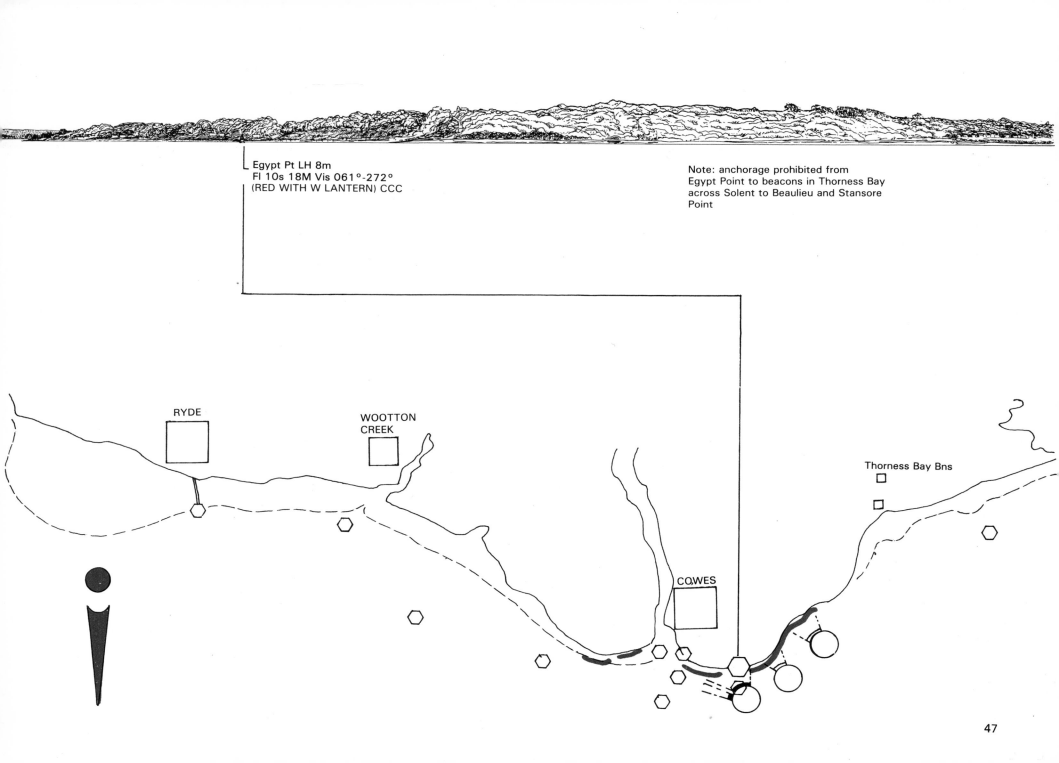

Egypt Pt LH 8m
Fl 10s 18M Vis 061°-272°
(RED WITH W LANTERN) CCC

Note: anchorage prohibited from
Egypt Point to beacons in Thorness Bay
across Solent to Beaulieu and Stansore
Point

RYDE

WOOTTON
CREEK

Thorness Bay Bns

COWES

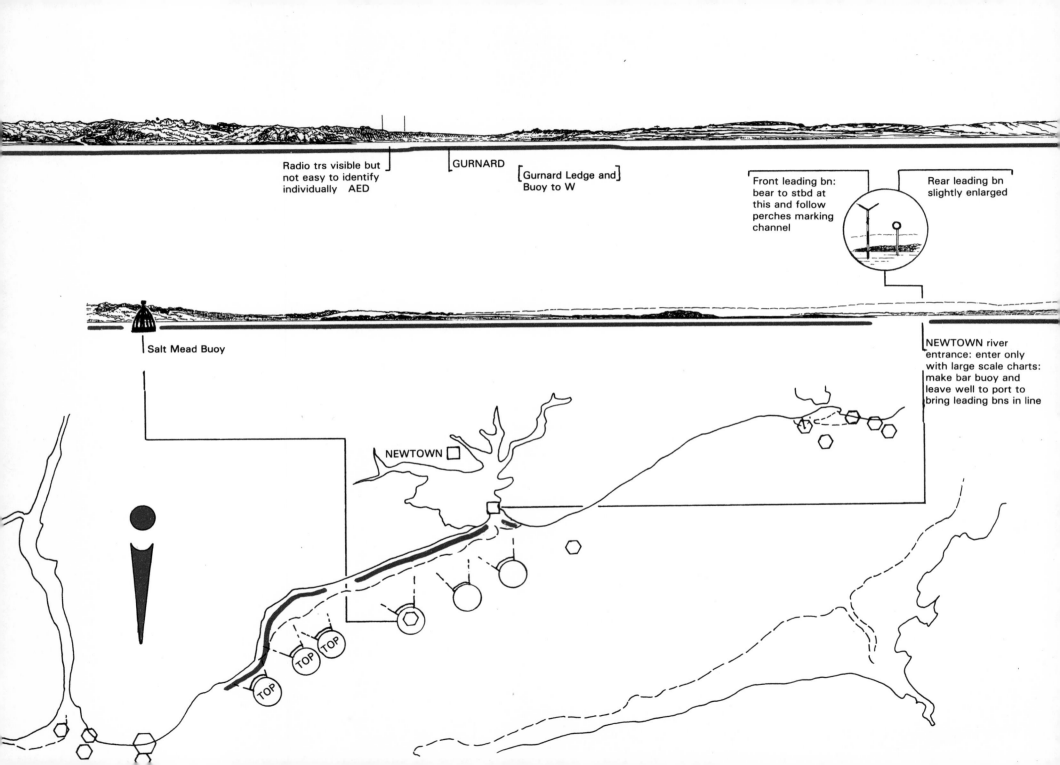

Radio trs visible but
not easy to identify
individually   AED

GURNARD

[Gurnard Ledge and]
Buoy to W

Front leading bn:
bear to stbd at
this and follow
perches marking
channel

Rear leading bn
slightly enlarged

Salt Mead Buoy

NEWTOWN river
entrance: enter only
with large scale charts:
make bar buoy and
leave well to port to
bring leading bns in line

NEWTOWN

TOP

TOP

TOP

TOP

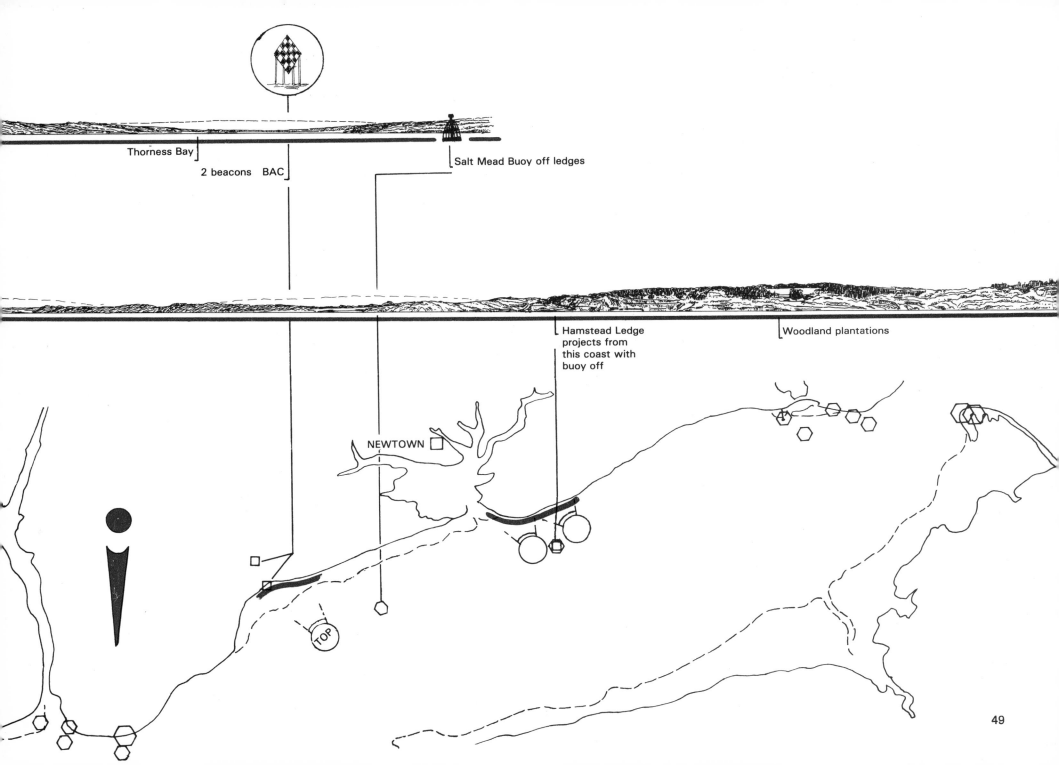

Thorness Bay

2 beacons BAC

Salt Mead Buoy off ledges

Hamstead Ledge
projects from
this coast with
buoy off

Woodland plantations

NEWTOWN

TOP

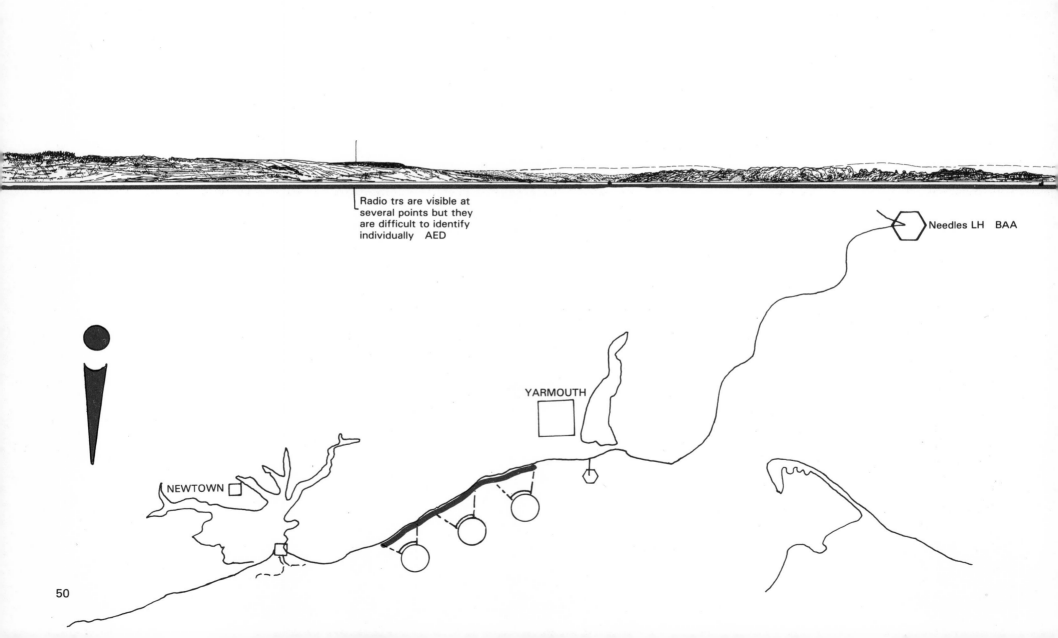

Radio trs are visible at
several points but they
are difficult to identify
individually   AED

Needles LH   BAA

YARMOUTH

NEWTOWN

50

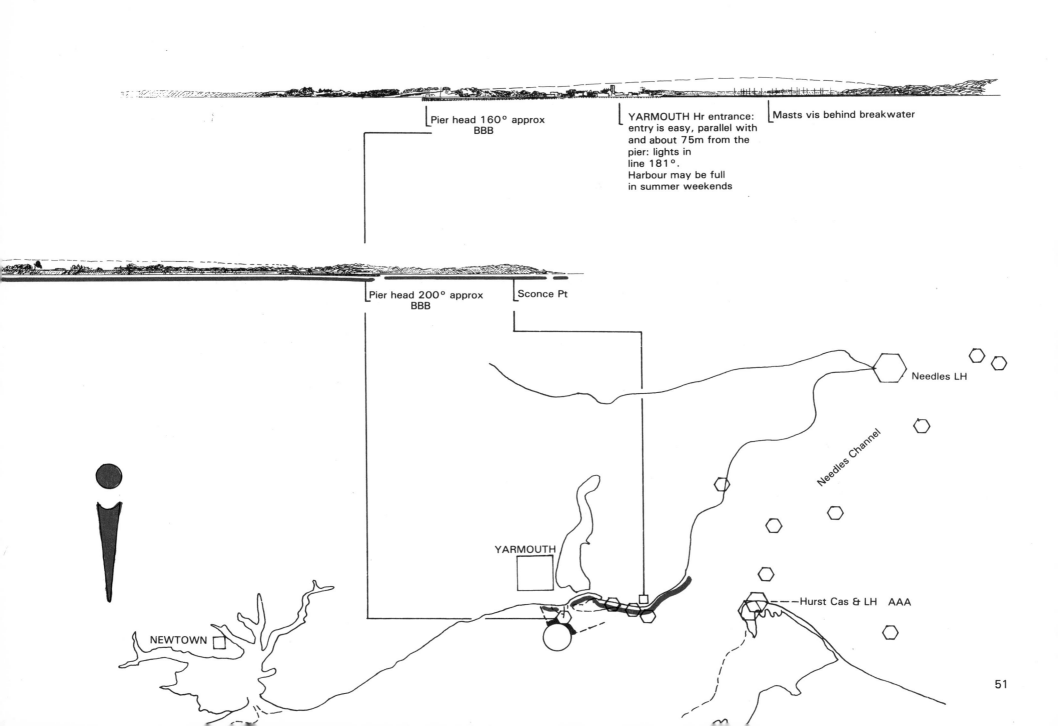

Pier head 160° approx
BBB

YARMOUTH Hr entrance:
entry is easy, parallel with
and about 75m from the
pier: lights in
line 181°.
Harbour may be full
in summer weekends

Masts vis behind breakwater

Pier head 200° approx
BBB

Sconce Pt

Needles LH

Needles Channel

YARMOUTH

Hurst Cas & LH   AAA

NEWTOWN

51

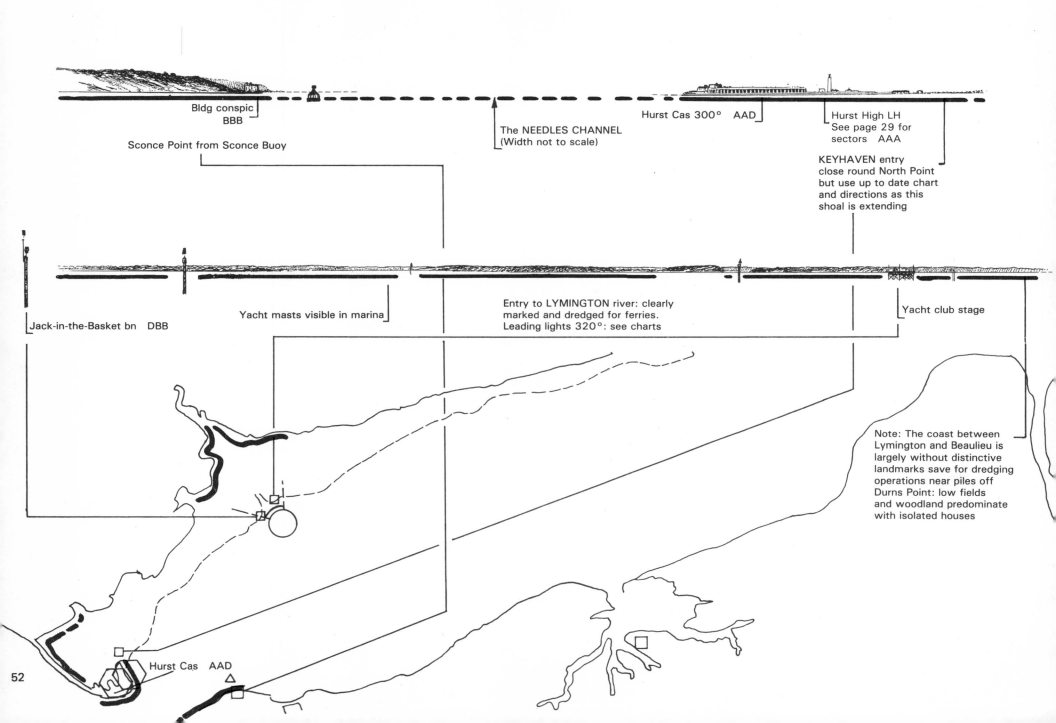

Bldg conspic
BBB

Sconce Point from Sconce Buoy

The NEEDLES CHANNEL
(Width not to scale)

Hurst Cas 300°   AAD

Hurst High LH
See page 29 for
sectors   AAA

KEYHAVEN entry
close round North Point
but use up to date chart
and directions as this
shoal is extending

Jack-in-the-Basket bn   DBB

Yacht masts visible in marina

Entry to LYMINGTON river: clearly
marked and dredged for ferries.
Leading lights 320°: see charts

Yacht club stage

Note: The coast between
Lymington and Beaulieu is
largely without distinctive
landmarks save for dredging
operations near piles off
Durns Point: low fields
and woodland predominate
with isolated houses

Hurst Cas   AAD

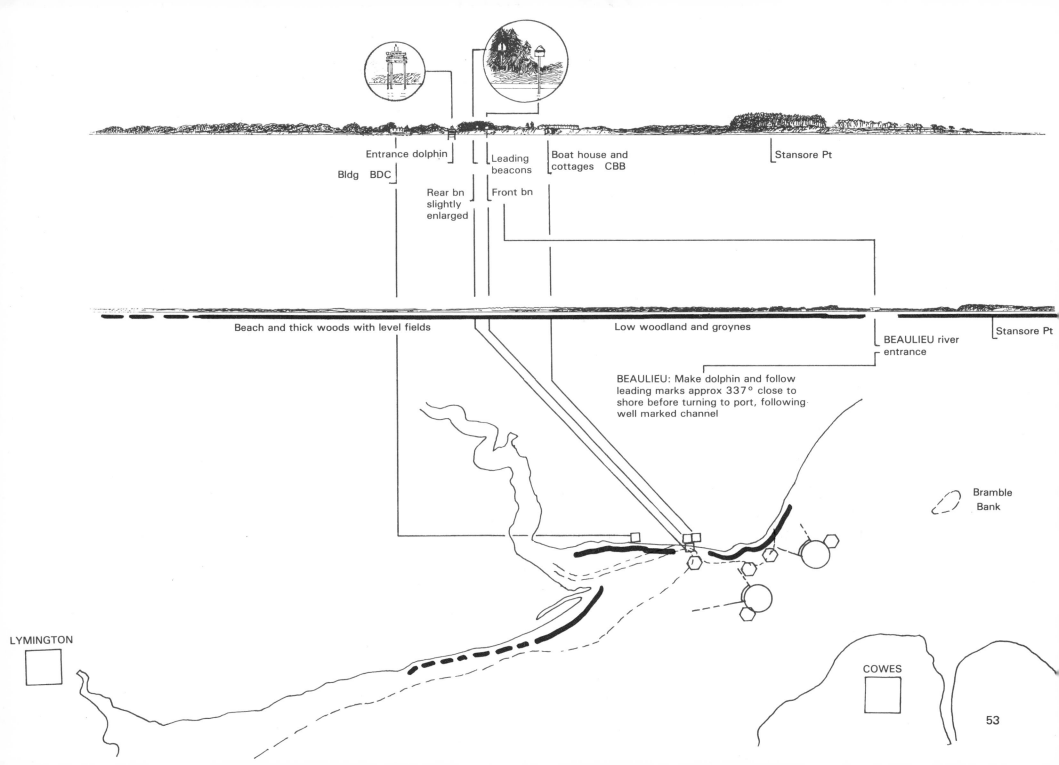

Entrance dolphin

Bldg BDC

Rear bn
slightly
enlarged

Leading
beacons

Front bn

Boat house and
cottages CBB

Stansore Pt

Beach and thick woods with level fields

Low woodland and groynes

Stansore Pt

BEAULIEU river
entrance

BEAULIEU: Make dolphin and follow
leading marks approx 337° close to
shore before turning to port, following
well marked channel

Bramble
Bank

LYMINGTON

COWES

53

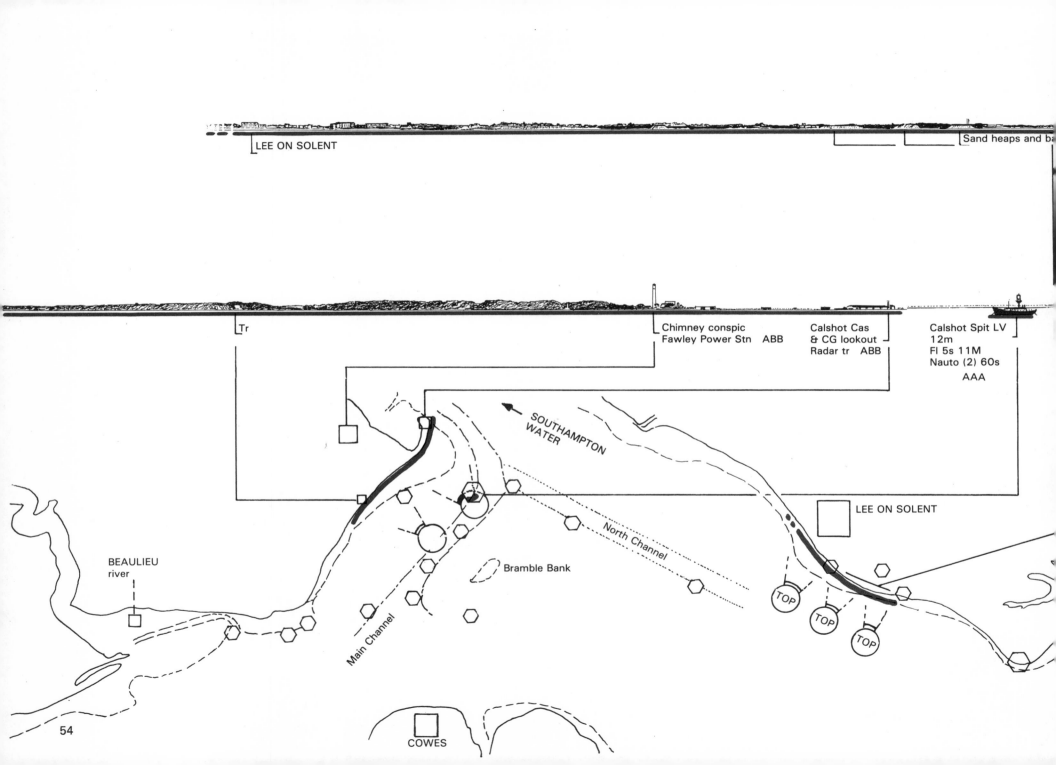

LEE ON SOLENT

Sand heaps and ba

Tr

Chimney conspic
Fawley Power Stn   ABB

Calshot Cas
& CG lookout
Radar tr   ABB

Calshot Spit LV
12m
Fl 5s 11M
Nauto (2) 60s
   AAA

SOUTHAMPTON
WATER

LEE ON SOLENT

North Channel

Bramble Bank

BEAULIEU
river

Main Channel

TOP

TOP

TOP

54

COWES

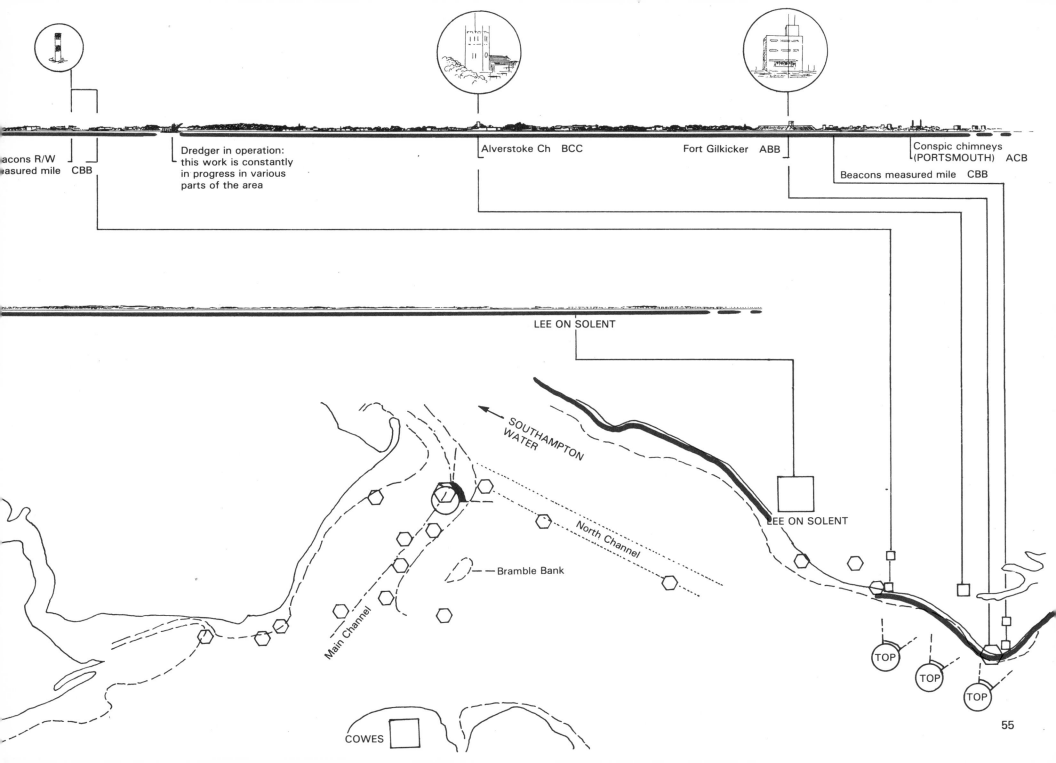

Beacons R/W
measured mile CBB

Dredger in operation:
this work is constantly
in progress in various
parts of the area

Alverstoke Ch BCC

Fort Gilkicker ABB

Conspic chimneys
(PORTSMOUTH) ACB

Beacons measured mile CBB

LEE ON SOLENT

SOUTHAMPTON
WATER

LEE ON SOLENT

North Channel

Bramble Bank

Main Channel

TOP

TOP

TOP

COWES

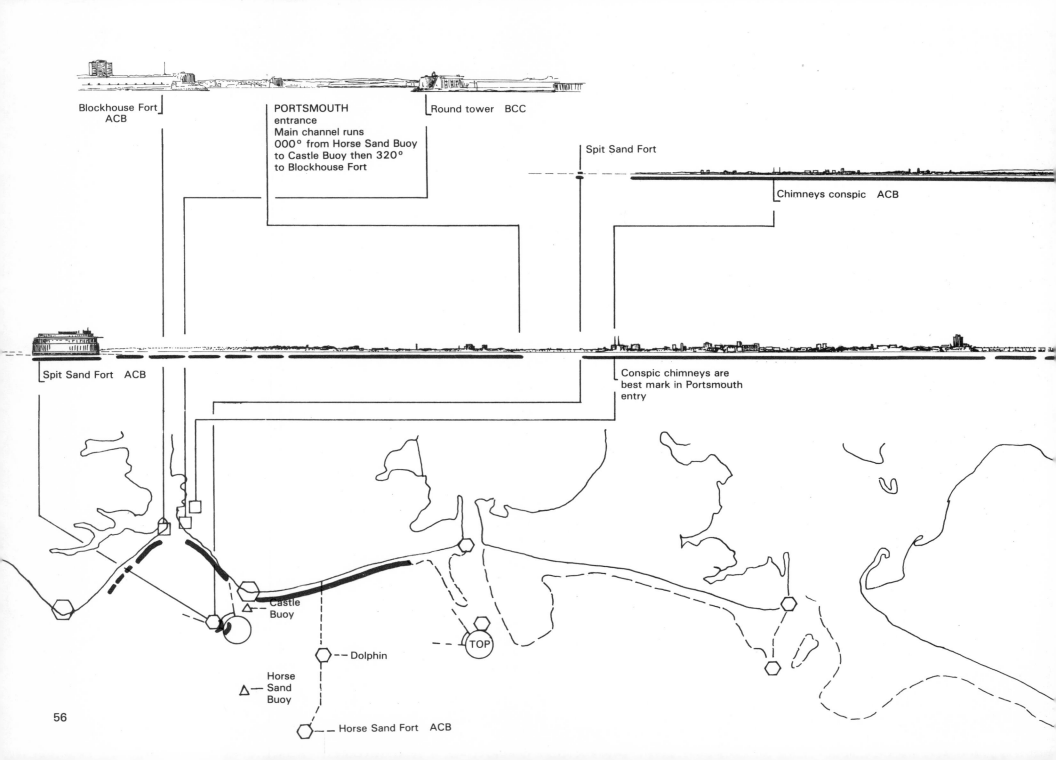

Blockhouse Fort
ACB

PORTSMOUTH
entrance
Main channel runs
000° from Horse Sand Buoy
to Castle Buoy then 320°
to Blockhouse Fort

Round tower   BCC

Spit Sand Fort

Chimneys conspic   ACB

Spit Sand Fort   ACB

Conspic chimneys are
best mark in Portsmouth
entry

Castle
Buoy

— Dolphin

TOP

Horse
Sand
Buoy

— Horse Sand Fort   ACB

56

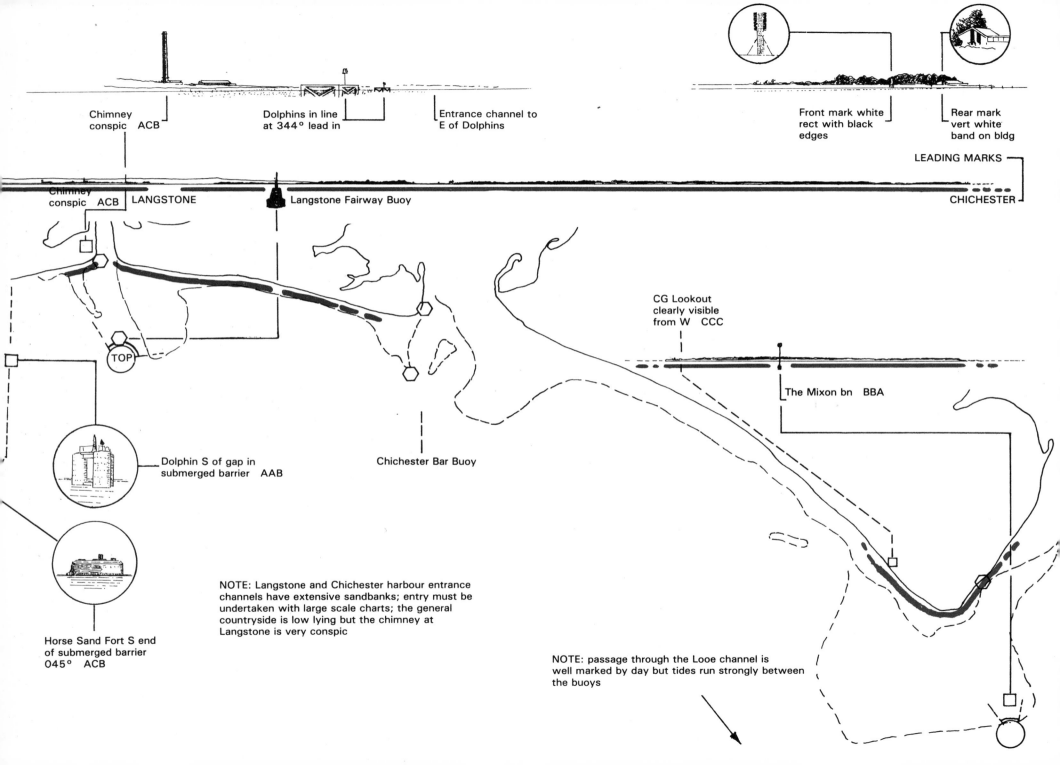

Chimney
conspic   ACB

Dolphins in line
at 344° lead in

Entrance channel to
E of Dolphins

Front mark white
rect with black
edges

Rear mark
vert white
band on bldg

LEADING MARKS

Chimney
conspic   ACB   LANGSTONE

Langstone Fairway Buoy

CHICHESTER

CG Lookout
clearly visible
from W   CCC

TOP

The Mixon bn   BBA

Dolphin S of gap in
submerged barrier   AAB

Chichester Bar Buoy

NOTE: Langstone and Chichester harbour entrance
channels have extensive sandbanks; entry must be
undertaken with large scale charts; the general
countryside is low lying but the chimney at
Langstone is very conspic

Horse Sand Fort S end
of submerged barrier
045°   ACB

NOTE: passage through the Looe channel is
well marked by day but tides run strongly between
the buoys

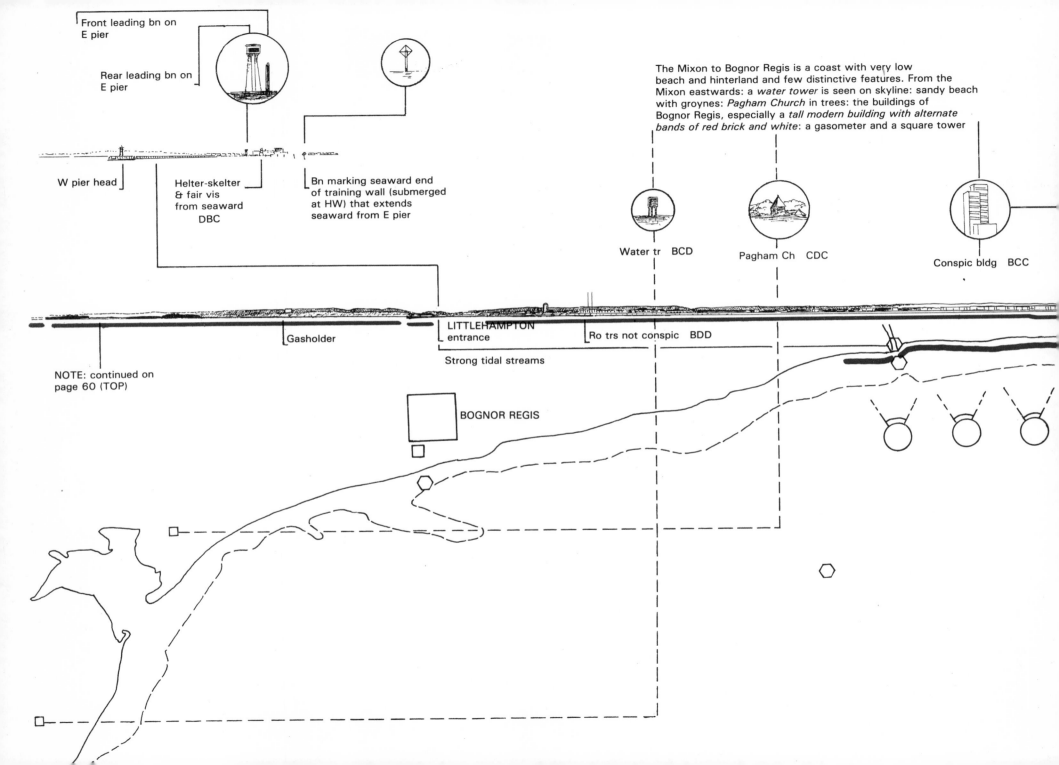

Front leading bn on
E pier

Rear leading bn on
E pier

W pier head

Helter-skelter
& fair vis
from seaward
DBC

Bn marking seaward end
of training wall (submerged
at HW) that extends
seaward from E pier

The Mixon to Bognor Regis is a coast with very low
beach and hinterland and few distinctive features. From the
Mixon eastwards: a *water tower* is seen on skyline: sandy beach
with groynes: *Pagham Church* in trees: the buildings of
Bognor Regis, especially a *tall modern building with alternate
bands of red brick and white*: a gasometer and a square tower

Water tr BCD

Pagham Ch CDC

Conspic bldg BCC

Gasholder

LITTLEHAMPTON
entrance

Ro trs not conspic BDD

Strong tidal streams

NOTE: continued on
page 60 (TOP)

BOGNOR REGIS

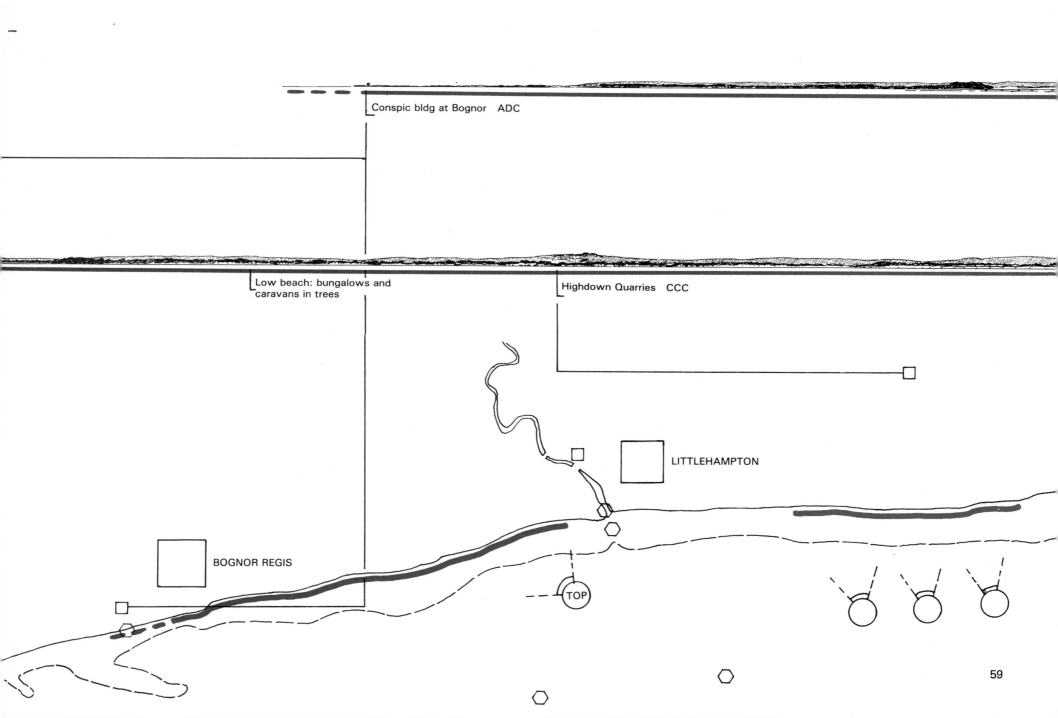

Conspic bldg at Bognor   ADC

Low beach: bungalows and
caravans in trees

Highdown Quarries   CCC

LITTLEHAMPTON

BOGNOR REGIS

TOP

59

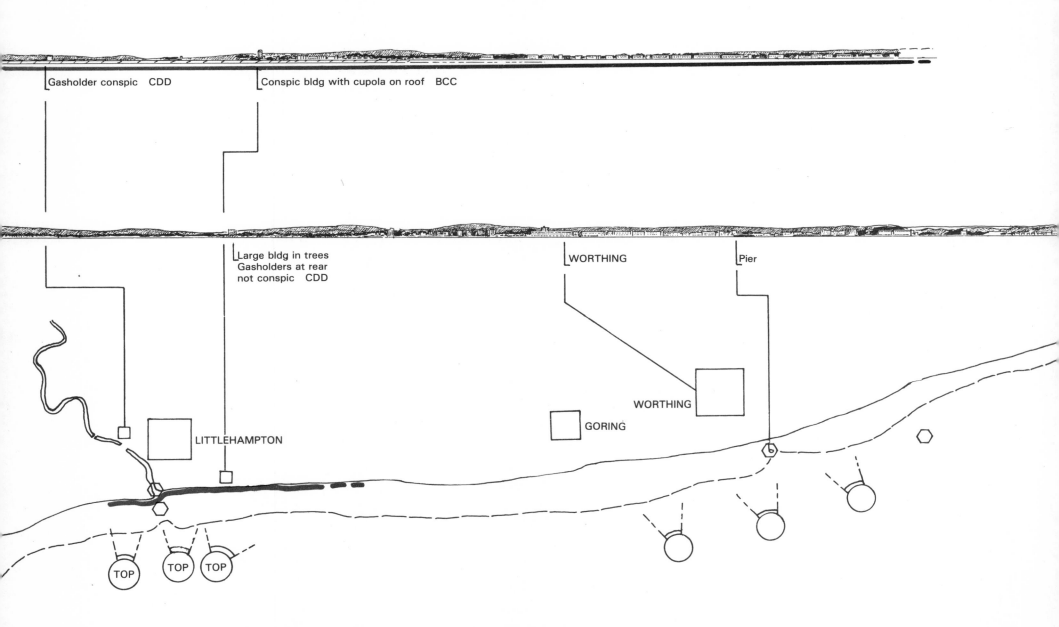

Gasholder conspic   CDD

Conspic bldg with cupola on roof   BCC

Large bldg in trees
Gasholders at rear
not conspic   CDD

WORTHING

Pier

WORTHING

GORING

LITTLEHAMPTON

TOP   TOP   TOP

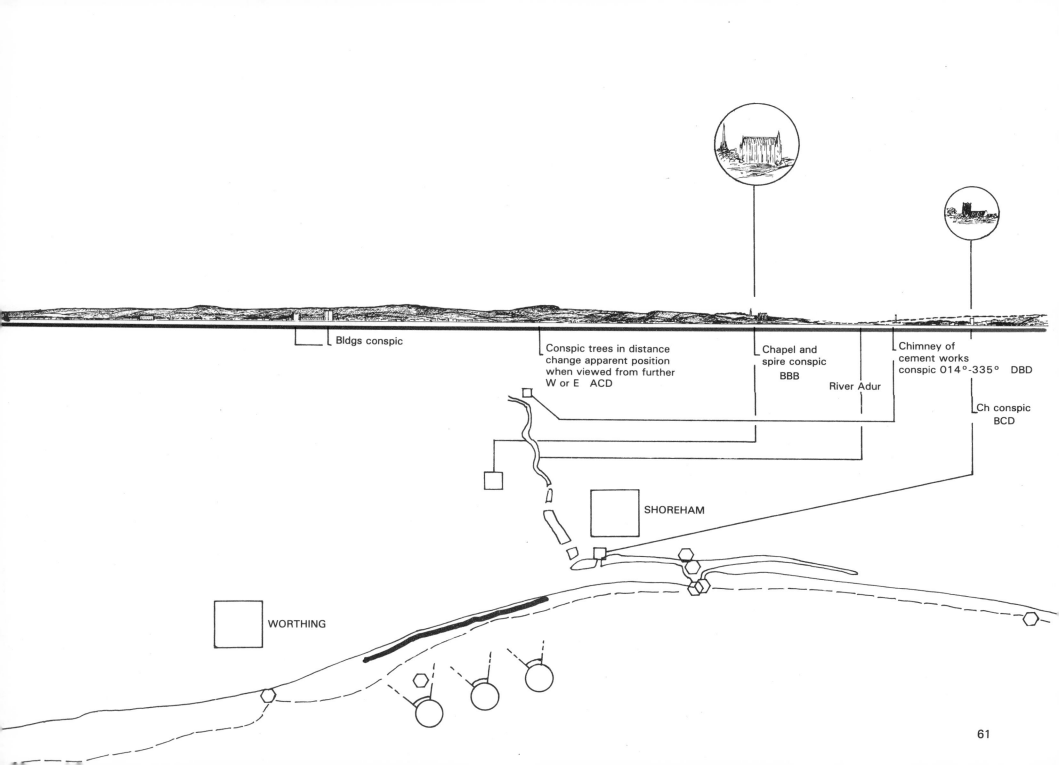

Bldgs conspic

Conspic trees in distance
change apparent position
when viewed from further
W or E   ACD

Chapel and
spire conspic
BBB

River Adur

Chimney of
cement works
conspic 014°-335°   DBD

Ch conspic
BCD

SHOREHAM

WORTHING

61

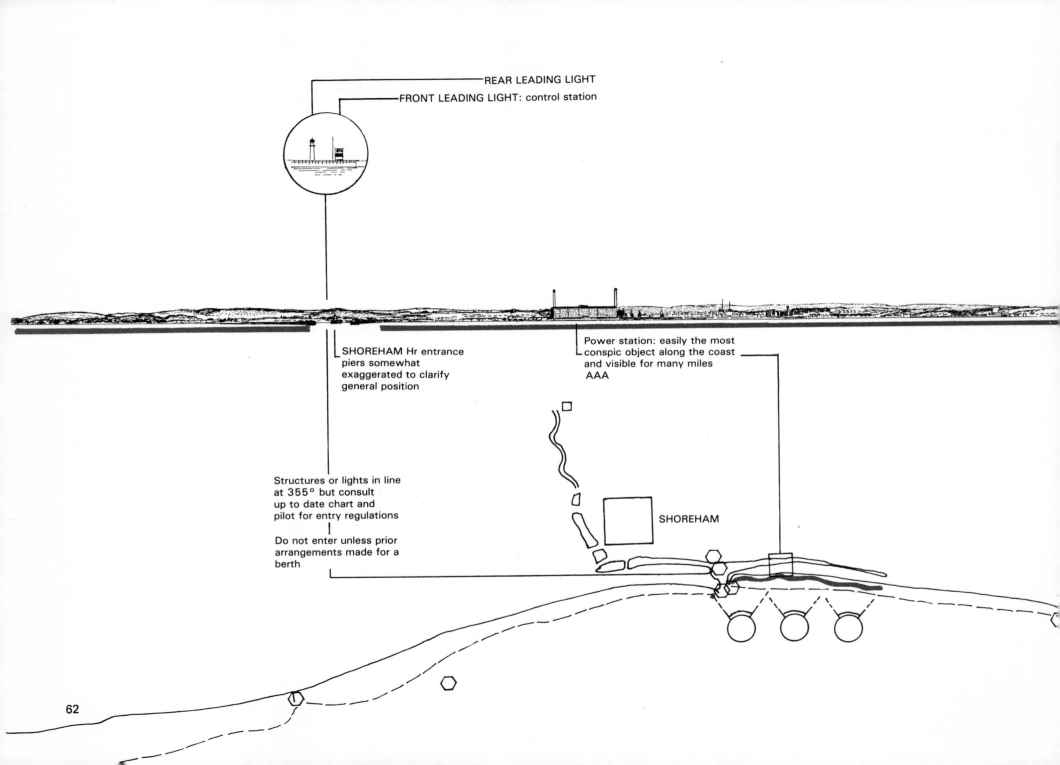

REAR LEADING LIGHT

FRONT LEADING LIGHT: control station

SHOREHAM Hr entrance
piers somewhat
exaggerated to clarify
general position

Power station: easily the most
conspic object along the coast
and visible for many miles
AAA

Structures or lights in line
at 355° but consult
up to date chart and
pilot for entry regulations

Do not enter unless prior
arrangements made for a
berth

SHOREHAM

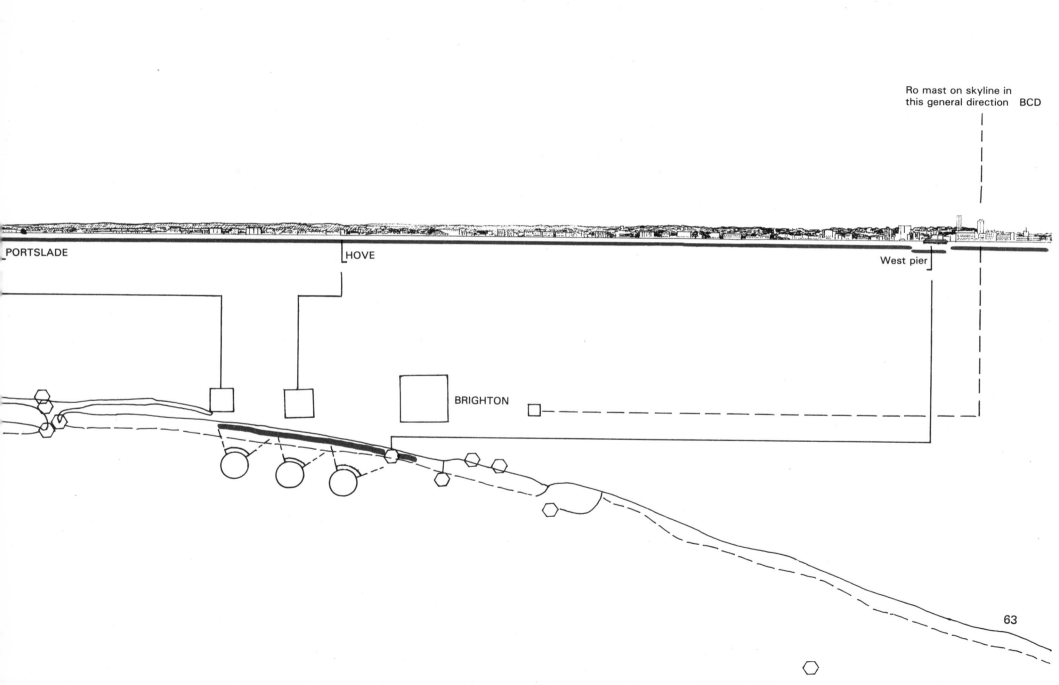

Ro mast on skyline in
this general direction BCD

PORTSLADE

HOVE

West pier

BRIGHTON

63

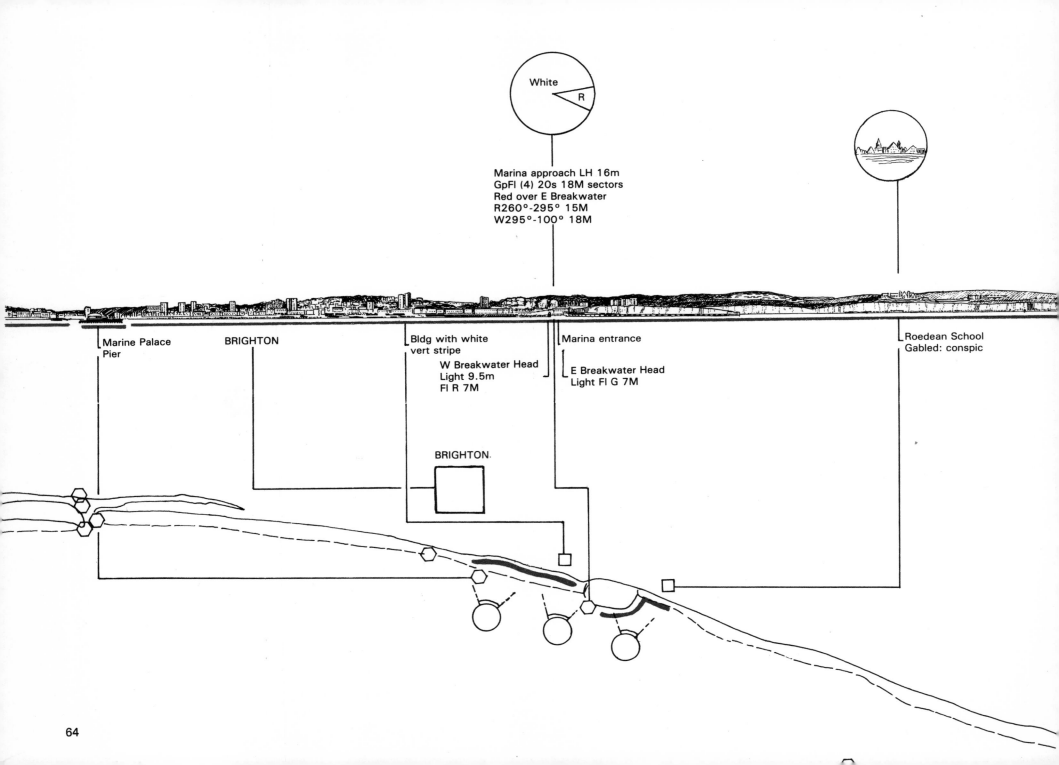

White

R

Marina approach LH 16m
GpFl (4) 20s 18M sectors
Red over E Breakwater
R260°-295° 15M
W295°-100° 18M

Marine Palace
Pier

BRIGHTON

Bldg with white
vert stripe

W Breakwater Head
Light 9.5m
Fl R 7M

Marina entrance

E Breakwater Head
Light Fl G 7M

Roedean School
Gabled: conspic

BRIGHTON.

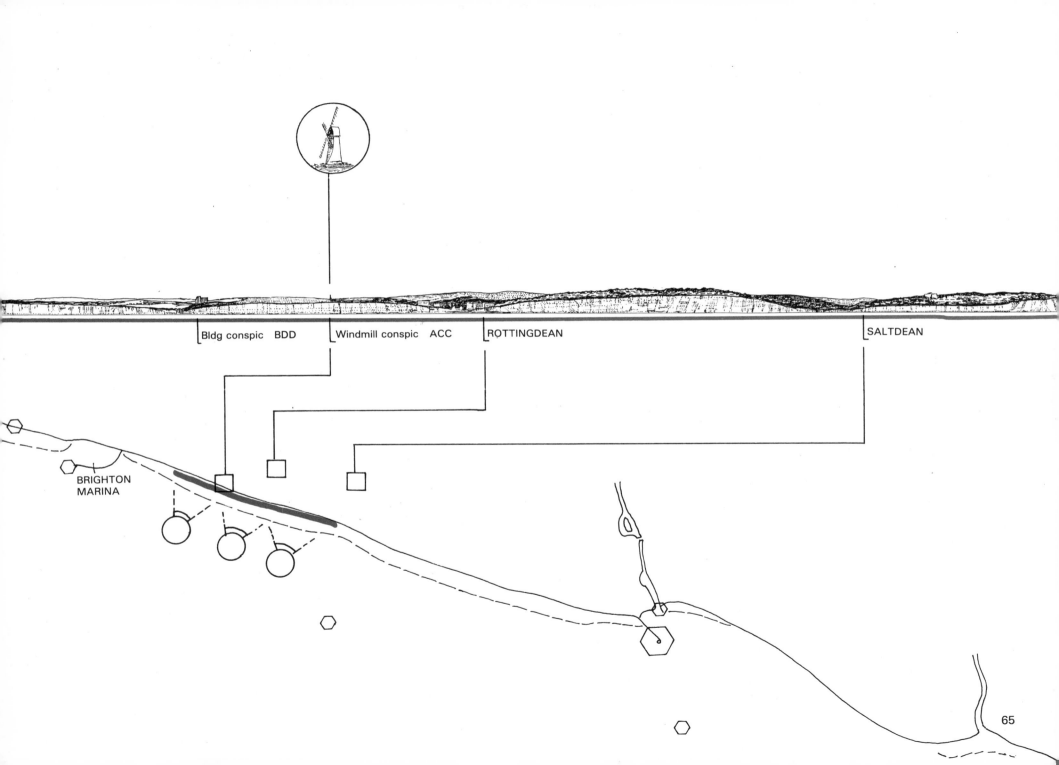

Bldg conspic BDD   Windmill conspic ACC   ROTTINGDEAN   SALTDEAN

BRIGHTON
MARINA

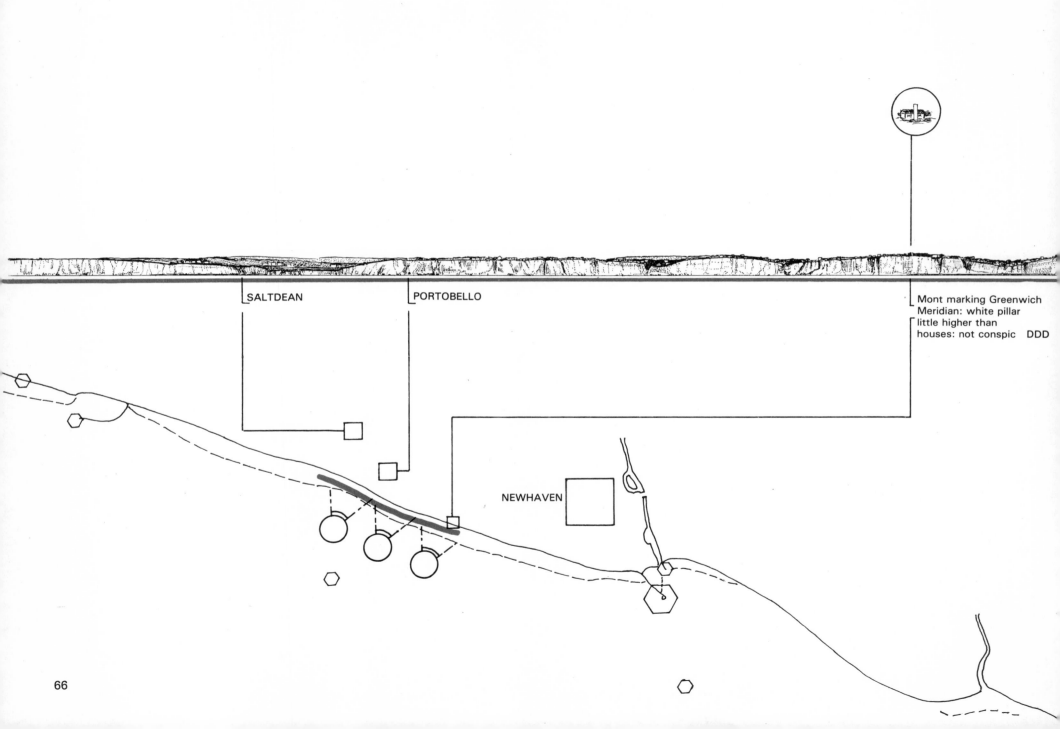

SALTDEAN

PORTOBELLO

Mont marking Greenwich
Meridian: white pillar
little higher than
houses: not conspic   DDD

NEWHAVEN

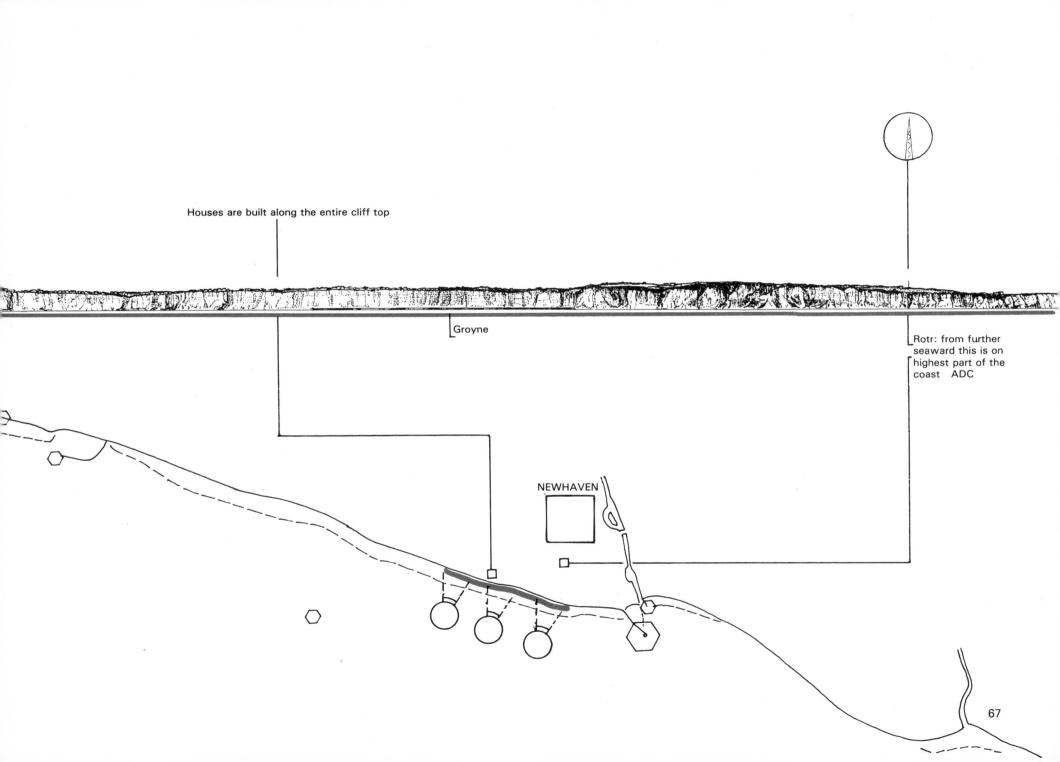

Houses are built along the entire cliff top

Groyne

Rotr: from further
seaward this is on
highest part of the
coast   ADC

NEWHAVEN

67

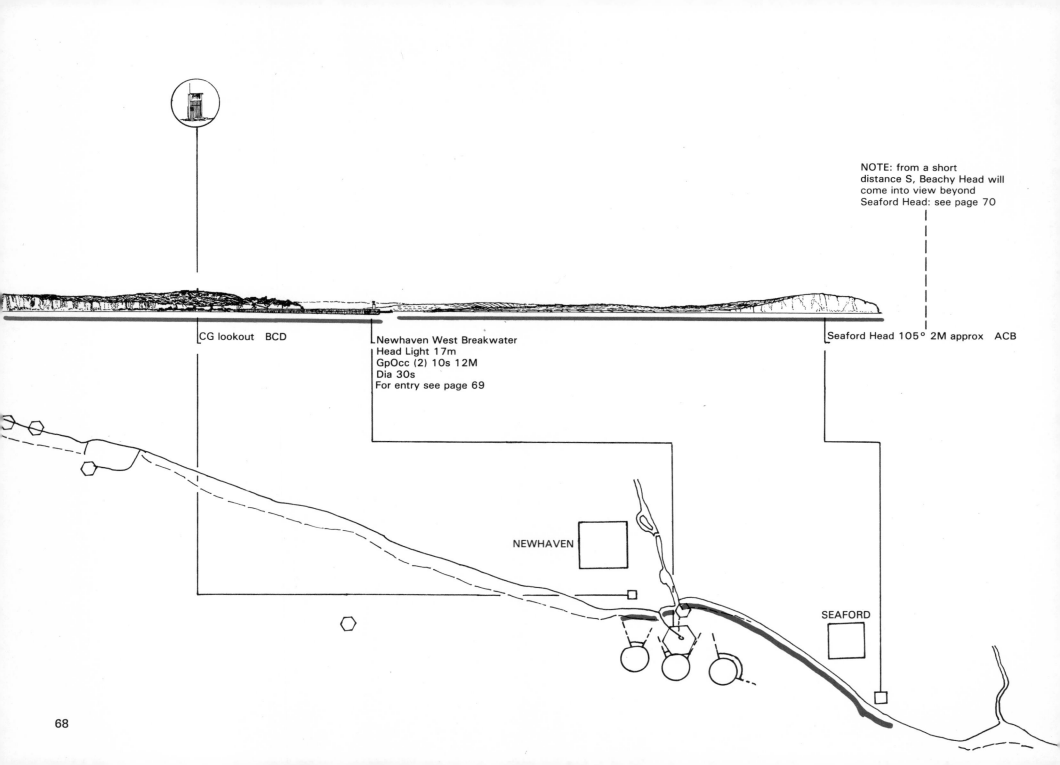

NOTE: from a short
distance S, Beachy Head will
come into view beyond
Seaford Head: see page 70

⌐CG lookout   BCD

⌐Newhaven West Breakwater
Head Light 17m
GpOcc (2) 10s 12M
Dia 30s
For entry see page 69

⌐Seaford Head 105° 2M approx   ACB

NEWHAVEN

SEAFORD

NEWHAVEN is easy to approach and enter, but previous arrangements for berthing in the marina or elsewhere should be made: boats berthing in the harbour itself face heavy charges except when sheltering from bad weather

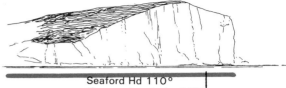

Seaford Hd 110°
(from a drawing)   ACB

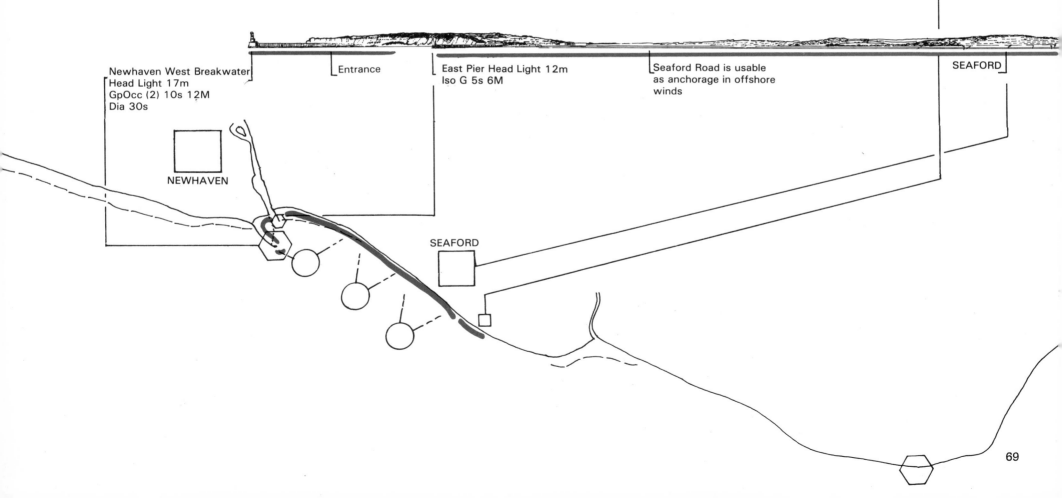

Newhaven West Breakwater
Head Light 17m
GpOcc (2) 10s 12M
Dia 30s

Entrance

East Pier Head Light 12m
Iso G 5s 6M

Seaford Road is usable
as anchorage in offshore
winds

SEAFORD

NEWHAVEN

SEAFORD

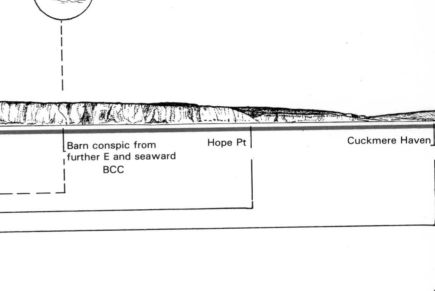

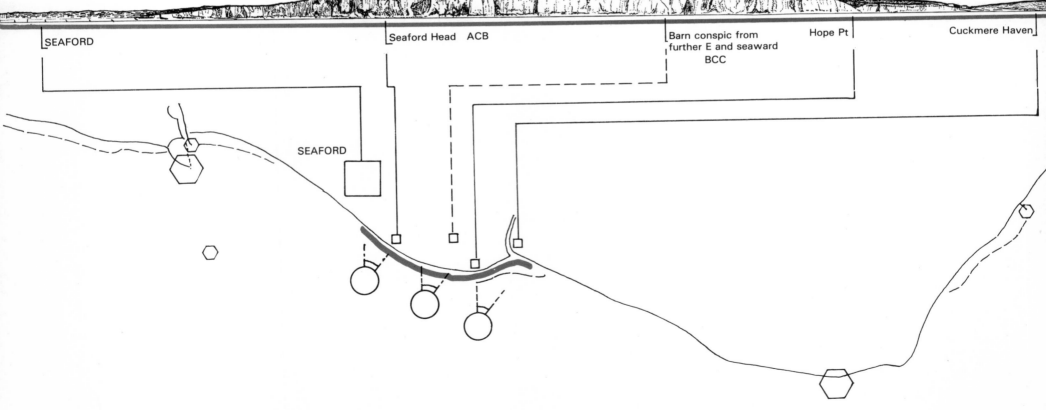

SEAFORD

Seaford Head   ACB

Barn conspic from
further E and seaward
BCC

Hope Pt

Cuckmere Haven

SEAFORD

70

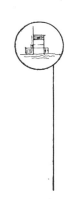

The Seven Sisters:
rounded cliffs from
Cuckmere to Beachy Hd,
Distinctive from West

Large grey house
in trees

Grey house

CG Lookout

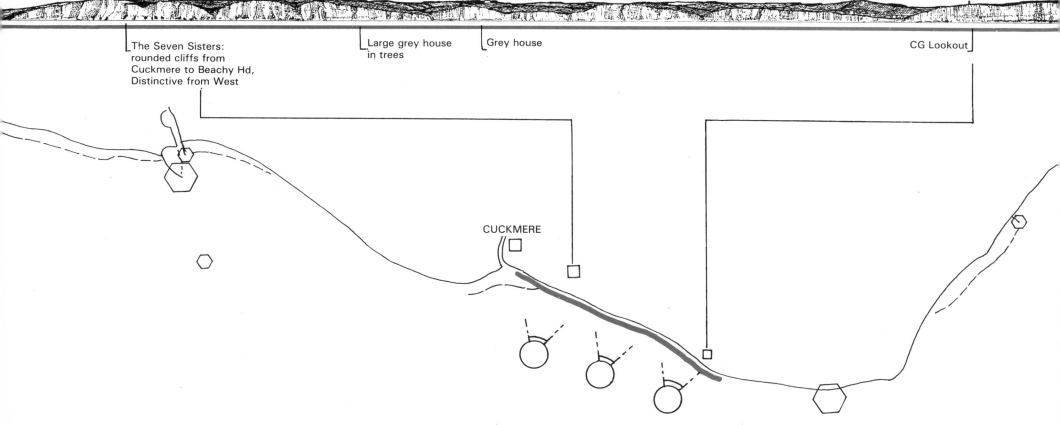

CUCKMERE

71

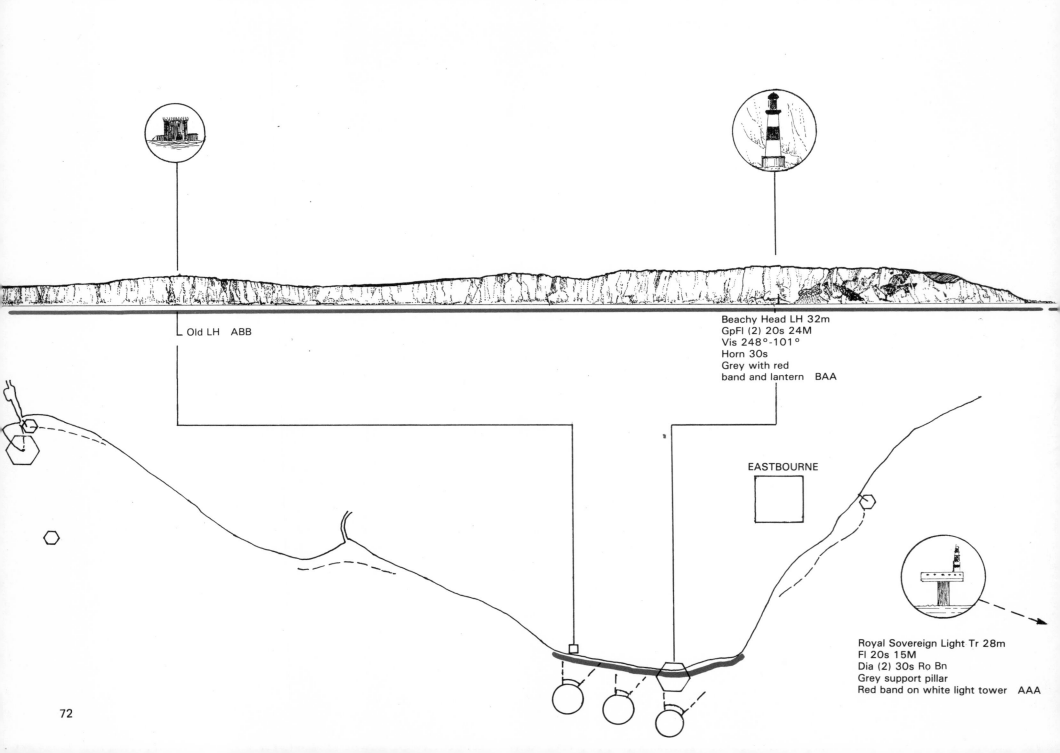

Old LH   ABB

Beachy Head LH 32m
GpFl (2) 20s 24M
Vis 248°-101°
Horn 30s
Grey with red
band and lantern   BAA

EASTBOURNE

Royal Sovereign Light Tr 28m
Fl 20s 15M
Dia (2) 30s Ro Bn
Grey support pillar
Red band on white light tower   AAA

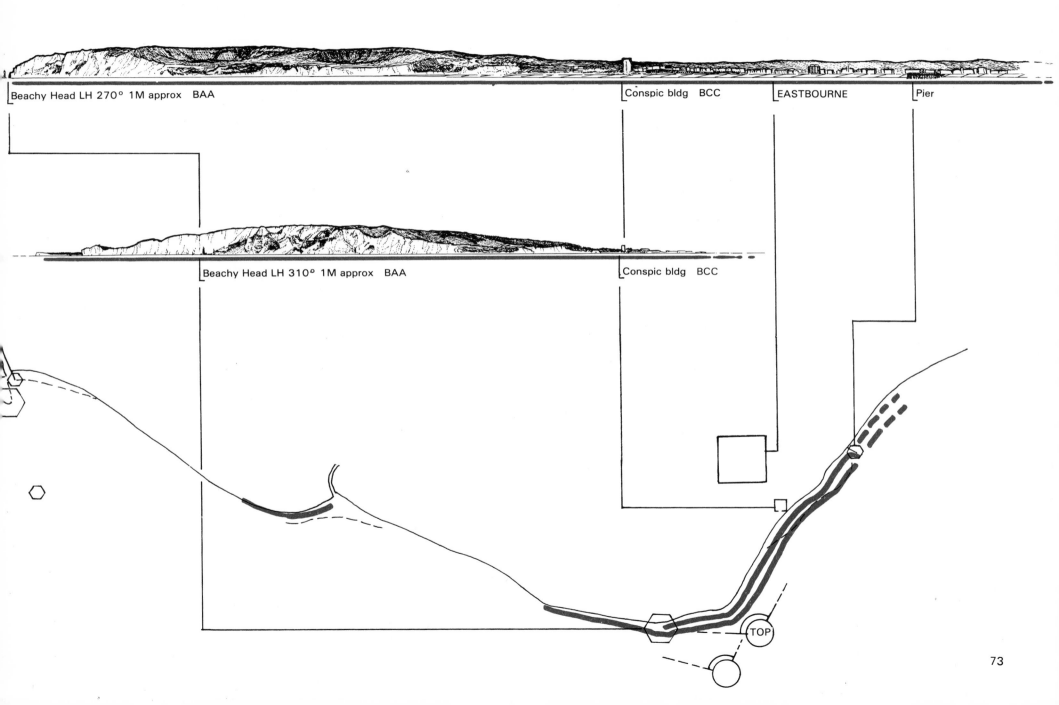

Beachy Head LH 270° 1M approx   BAA   Conspic bldg   BCC   EASTBOURNE   Pier

Beachy Head LH 310° 1M approx   BAA   Conspic bldg   BCC

TOP

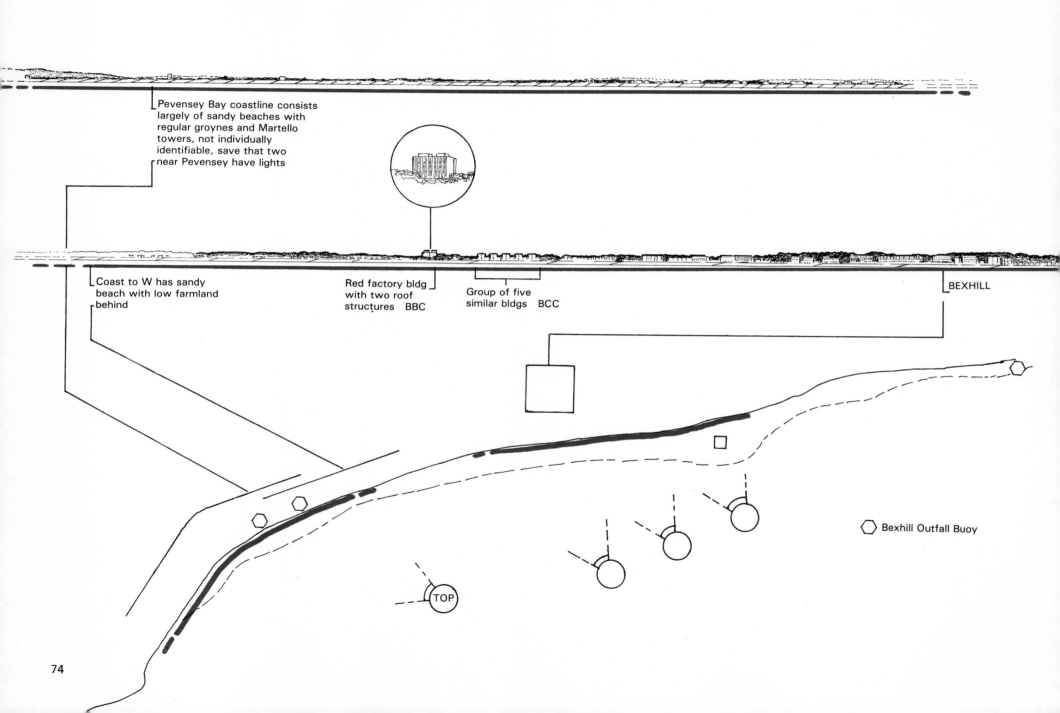

Pevensey Bay coastline consists
largely of sandy beaches with
regular groynes and Martello
towers, not individually
identifiable, save that two
near Pevensey have lights

Coast to W has sandy
beach with low farmland
behind

Red factory bldg
with two roof
structures   BBC

Group of five
similar bldgs   BCC

BEXHILL

TOP

⬡ Bexhill Outfall Buoy

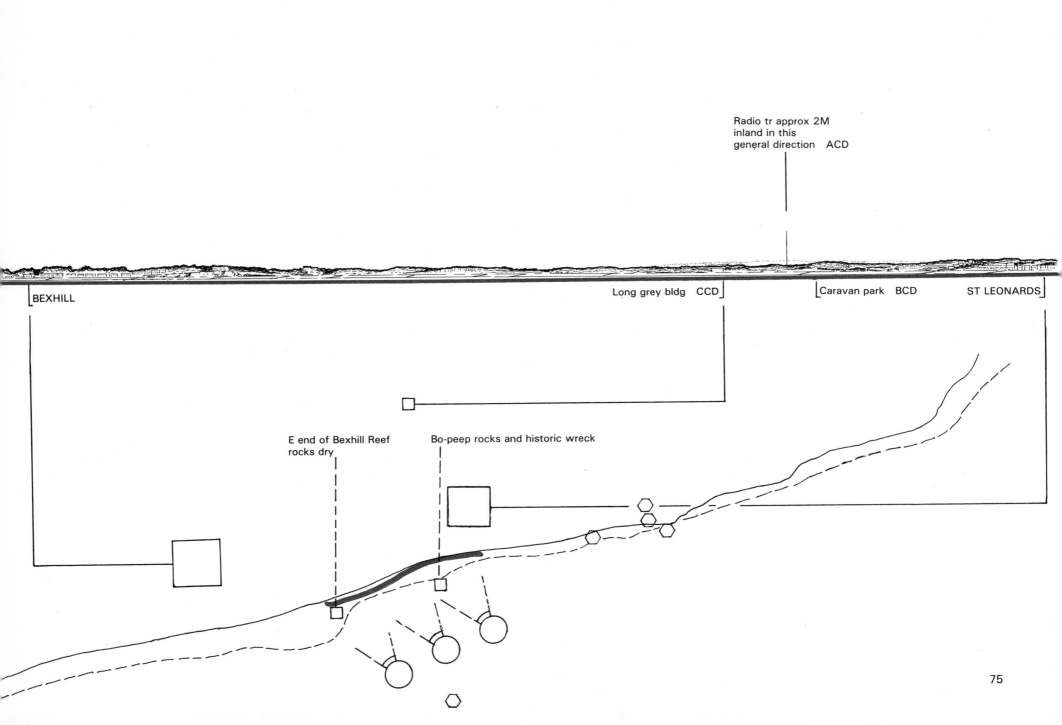

Radio tr approx 2M
inland in this
general direction   ACD

Long grey bldg   CCD

Caravan park   BCD

ST LEONARDS

BEXHILL

E end of Bexhill Reef
rocks dry

Bo-peep rocks and historic wreck

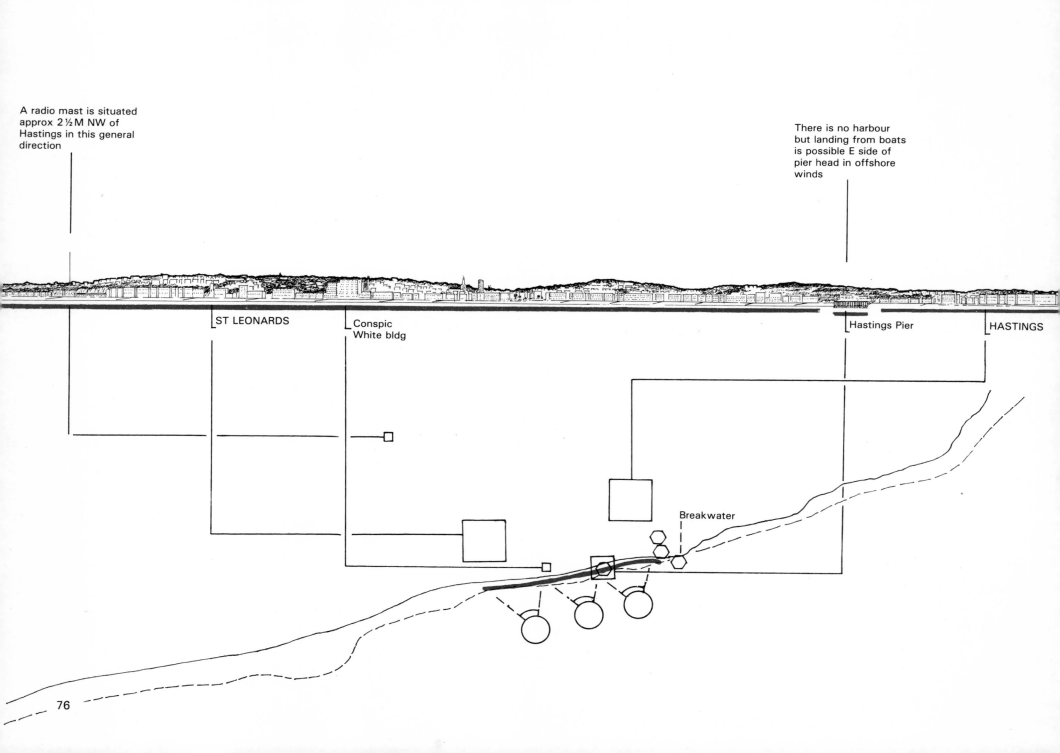

A radio mast is situated approx 2½M NW of Hastings in this general direction

There is no harbour but landing from boats is possible E side of pier head in offshore winds

ST LEONARDS

Conspic White bldg

Hastings Pier

HASTINGS

Breakwater

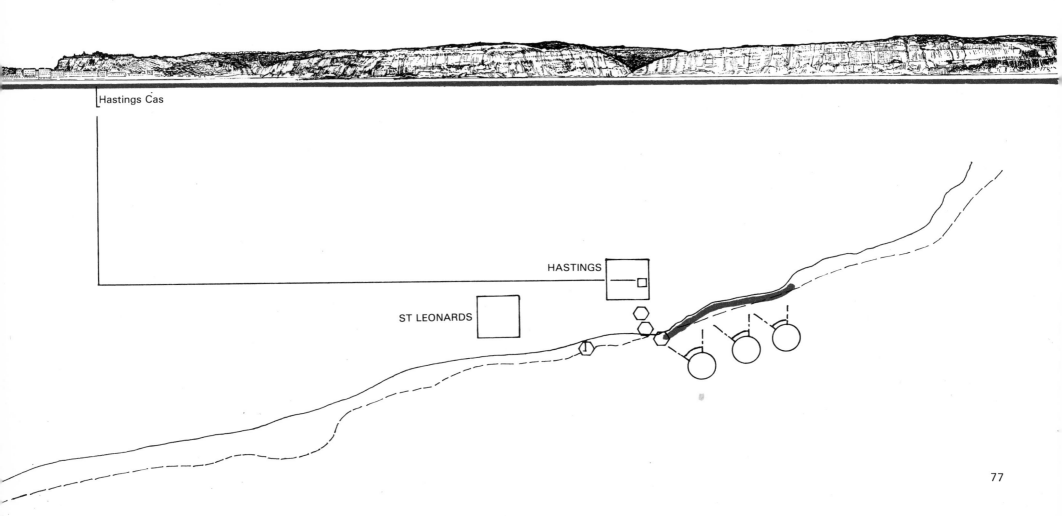

Hastings Cas

HASTINGS

ST LEONARDS

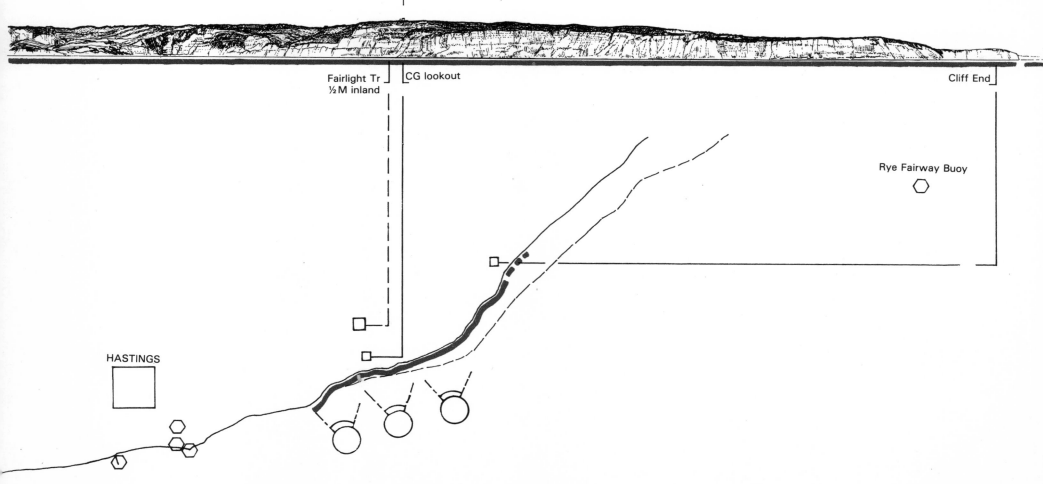

Fairlight Tr
½ M inland

CG lookout

Cliff End

Rye Fairway Buoy

HASTINGS

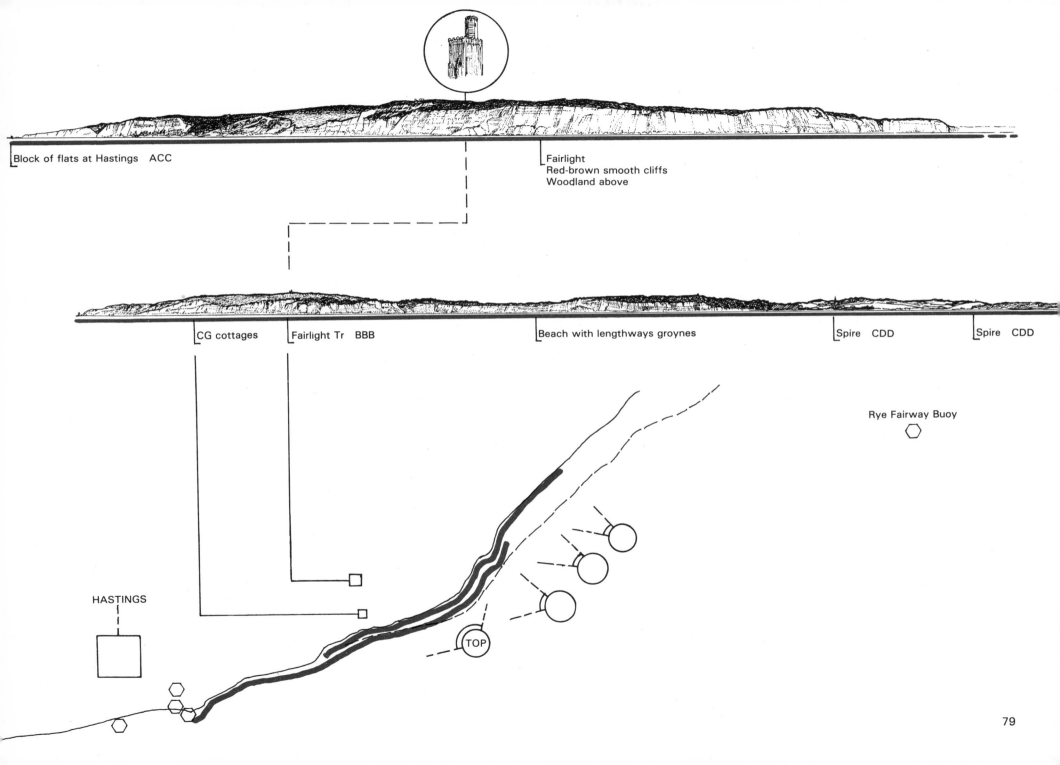

Block of flats at Hastings   ACC

Fairlight
Red-brown smooth cliffs
Woodland above

CG cottages   Fairlight Tr   BBB   Beach with lengthways groynes   Spire   CDD   Spire   CDD

Rye Fairway Buoy

HASTINGS

TOP

79

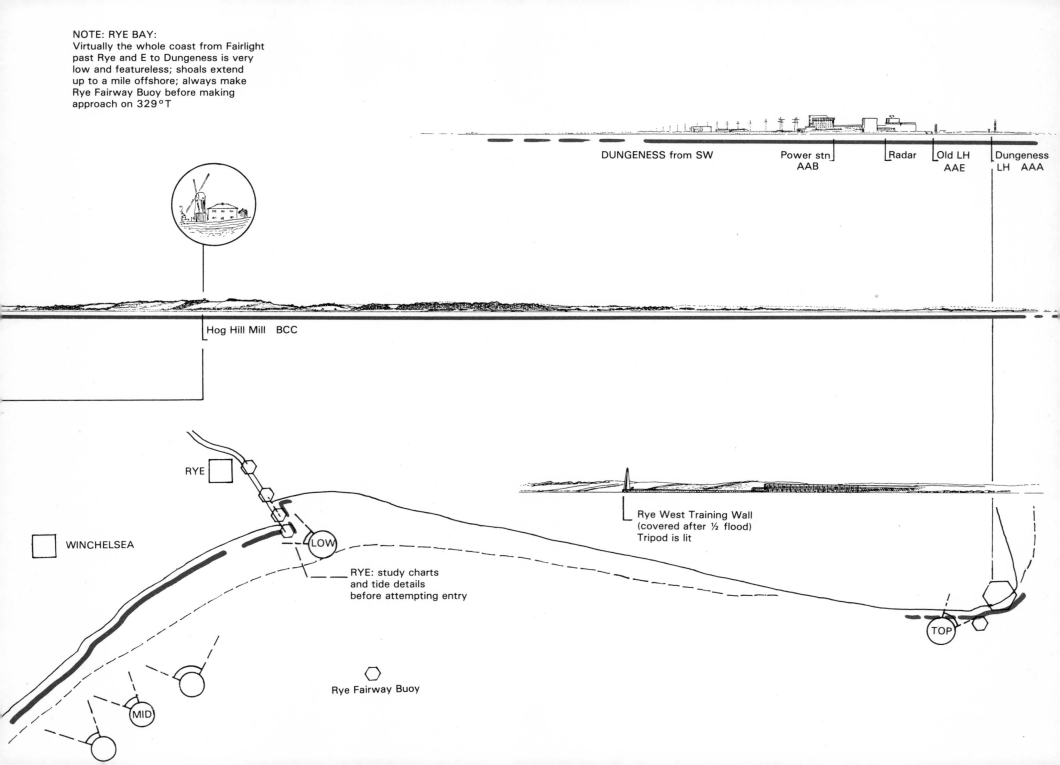

NOTE: RYE BAY:
Virtually the whole coast from Fairlight
past Rye and E to Dungeness is very
low and featureless; shoals extend
up to a mile offshore; always make
Rye Fairway Buoy before making
approach on 329°T

DUNGENESS from SW

Power stn
AAB

Radar

Old LH
AAE

Dungeness
LH AAA

Hog Hill Mill BCC

RYE

WINCHELSEA

LOW

RYE: study charts
and tide details
before attempting entry

Rye West Training Wall
(covered after ½ flood)
Tripod is lit

TOP

MID

Rye Fairway Buoy

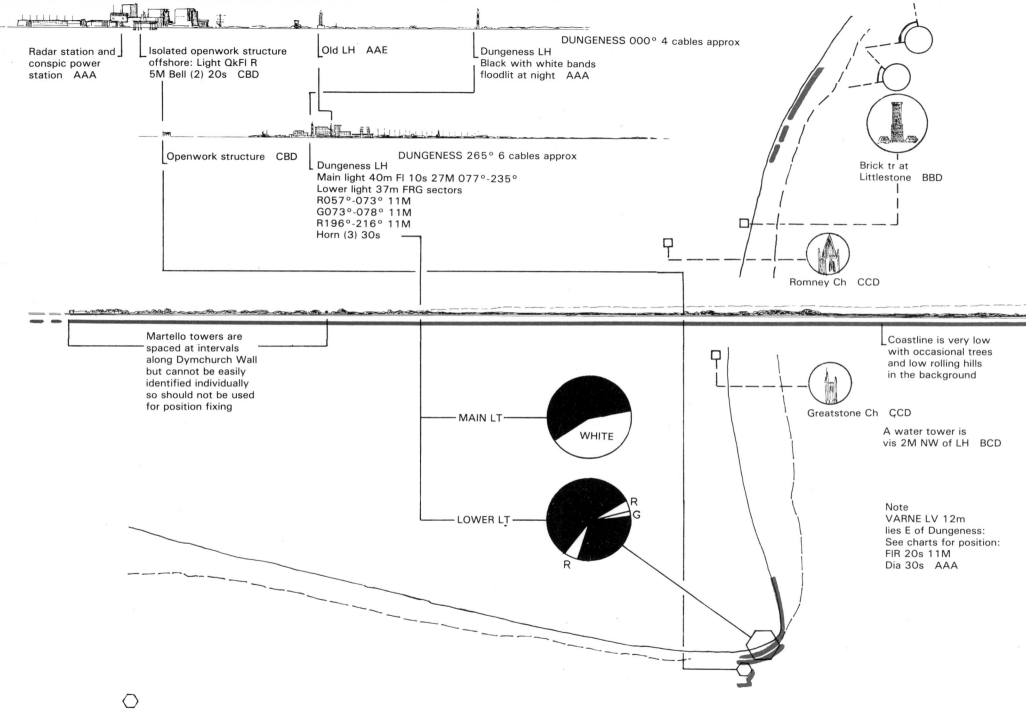

Radar station and conspic power station AAA

Isolated openwork structure offshore: Light QkFl R 5M Bell (2) 20s CBD

Old LH AAE

Dungeness LH Black with white bands floodlit at night AAA

DUNGENESS 000° 4 cables approx

Openwork structure CBD

Dungeness LH
Main light 40m Fl 10s 27M 077°-235°
Lower light 37m FRG sectors
R057°-073° 11M
G073°-078° 11M
R196°-216° 11M
Horn (3) 30s

DUNGENESS 265° 6 cables approx

Brick tr at Littlestone BBD

Romney Ch CCD

Martello towers are spaced at intervals along Dymchurch Wall but cannot be easily identified individually so should not be used for position fixing

Coastline is very low with occasional trees and low rolling hills in the background

MAIN LT — WHITE

LOWER LT — R G R

Greatstone Ch CCD

A water tower is vis 2M NW of LH BCD

Note
VARNE LV 12m
lies E of Dungeness:
See charts for position:
Fl R 20s 11M
Dia 30s AAA

81

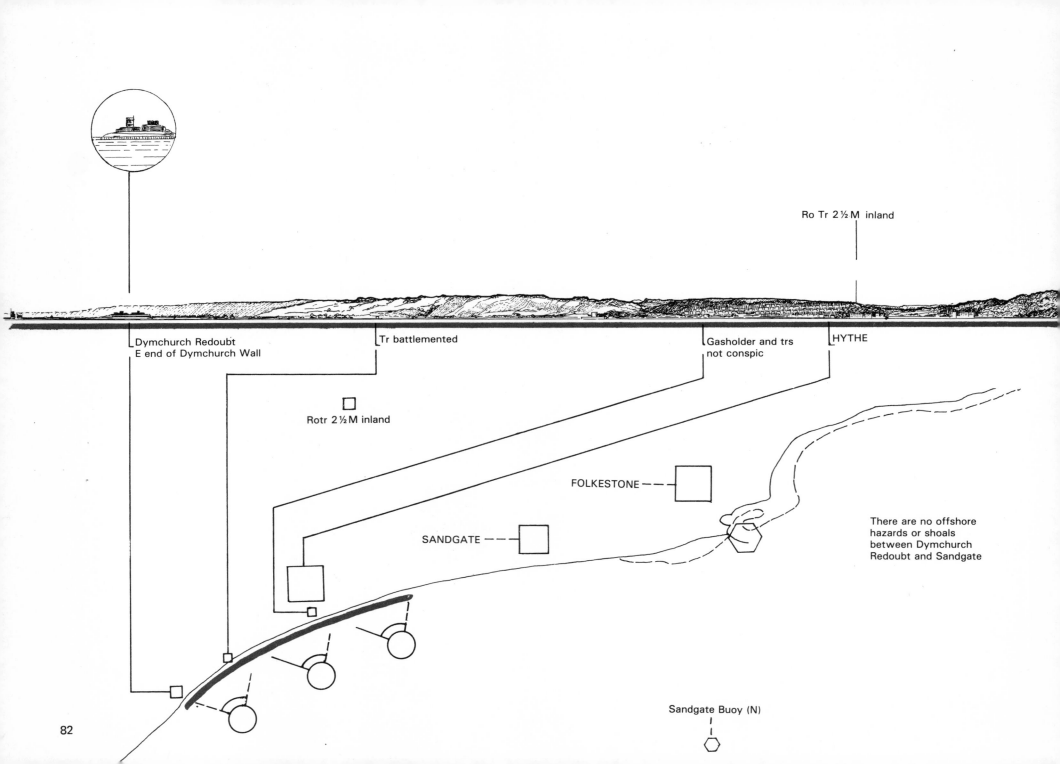

Ro Tr 2½ M inland

Dymchurch Redoubt
E end of Dymchurch Wall

Tr battlemented

Gasholder and trs
not conspic

HYTHE

Rotr 2½ M inland

FOLKESTONE

SANDGATE

There are no offshore
hazards or shoals
between Dymchurch
Redoubt and Sandgate

Sandgate Buoy (N)

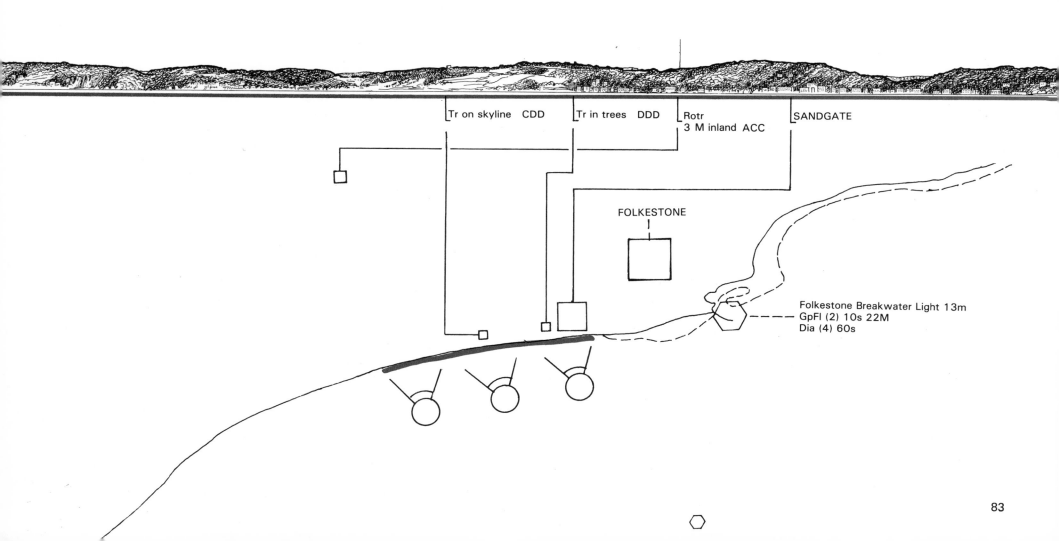

Tr on skyline CDD

Tr in trees DDD

Rotr
3 M inland ACC

SANDGATE

FOLKESTONE

Folkestone Breakwater Light 13m
GpFl (2) 10s 22M
Dia (4) 60s

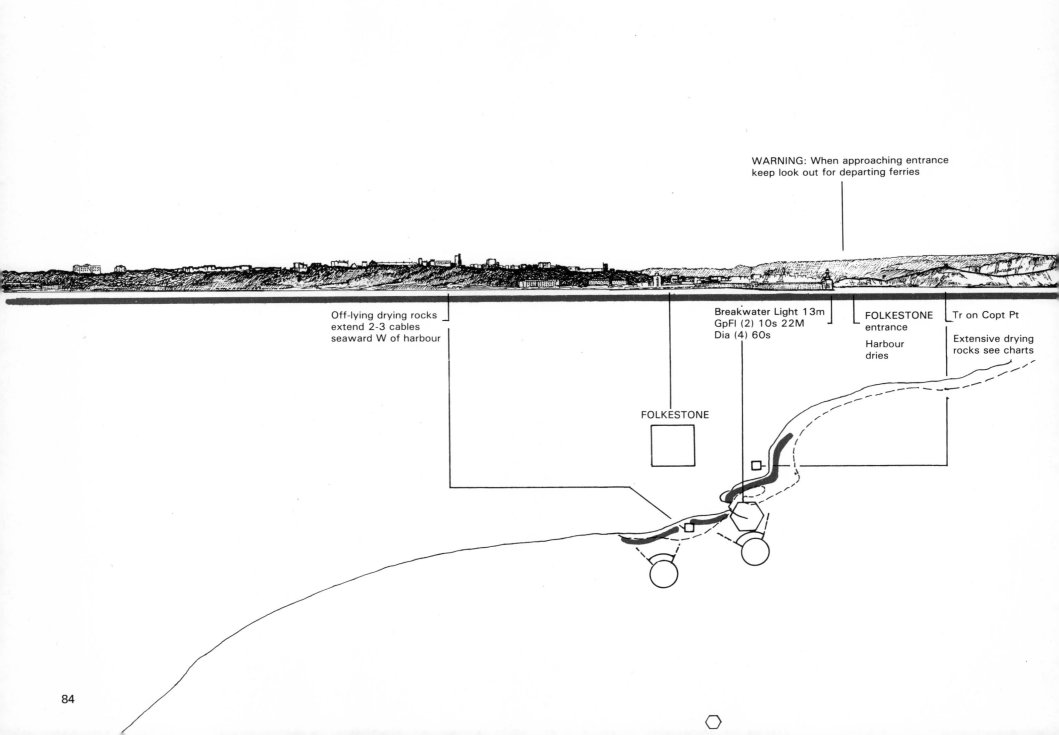

WARNING: When approaching entrance
keep look out for departing ferries

Off-lying drying rocks
extend 2-3 cables
seaward W of harbour

Breakwater Light 13m
GpFl (2) 10s 22M
Dia (4) 60s

FOLKESTONE
entrance

Harbour
dries

Tr on Copt Pt

Extensive drying
rocks see charts

FOLKESTONE

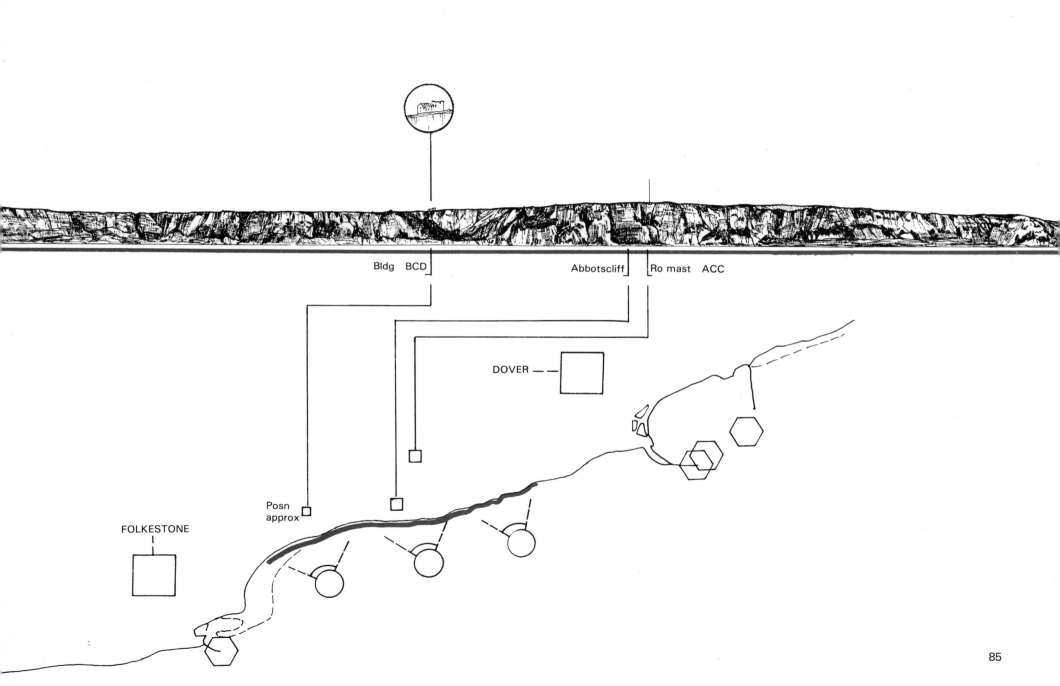

Bldg BCD

Abbotscliff Ro mast ACC

DOVER

Posn
approx

FOLKESTONE

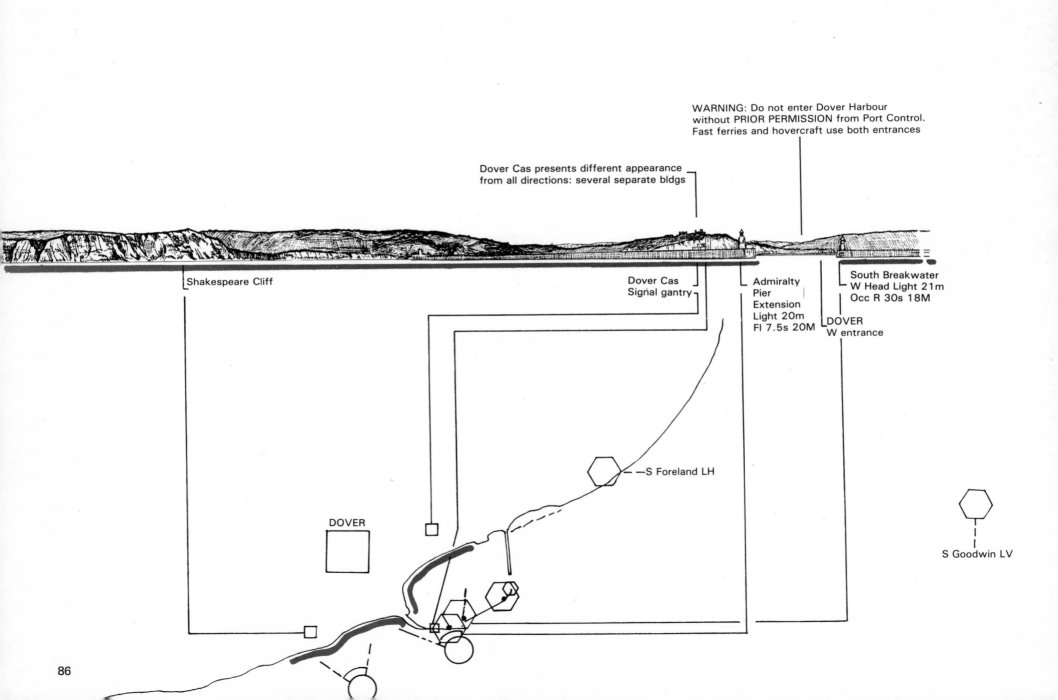

WARNING: Do not enter Dover Harbour
without PRIOR PERMISSION from Port Control.
Fast ferries and hovercraft use both entrances

Dover Cas presents different appearance
from all directions: several separate bldgs

Shakespeare Cliff

Dover Cas
Signal gantry

Admiralty
Pier
Extension
Light 20m
Fl 7.5s 20M

DOVER
W entrance

South Breakwater
W Head Light 21m
Occ R 30s 18M

S Foreland LH

DOVER

S Goodwin LV

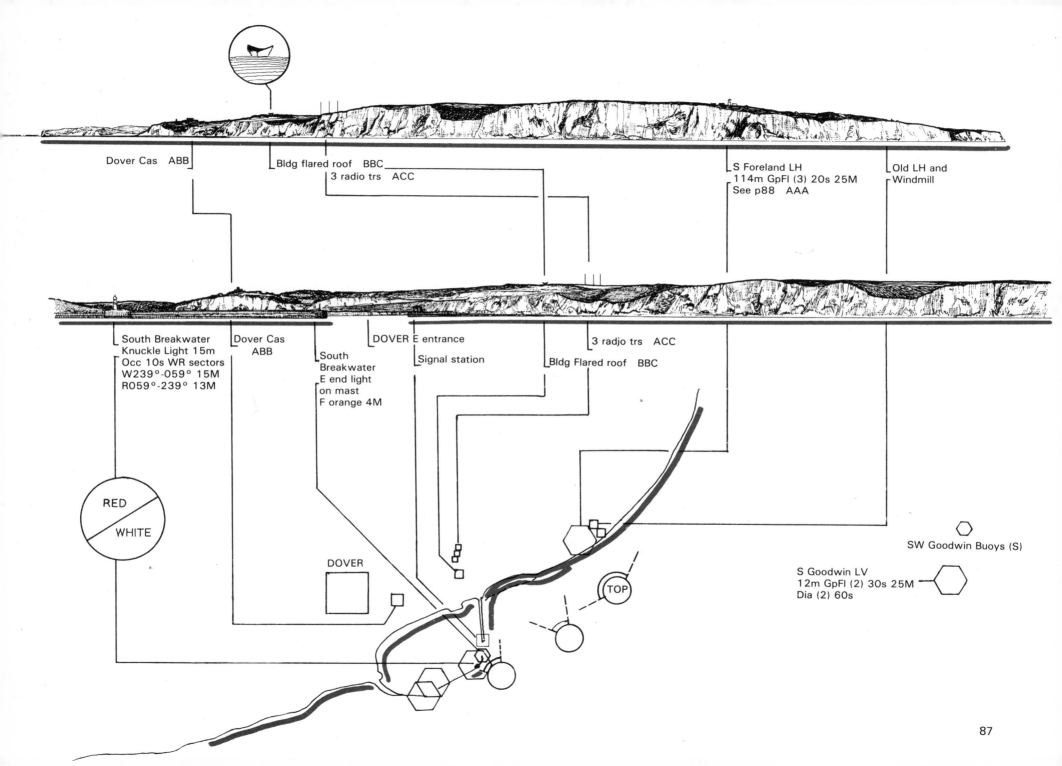

Dover Cas ABB

Bldg flared roof BBC
3 radio trs ACC

S Foreland LH
114m GpFl (3) 20s 25M
See p88 AAA

Old LH and
Windmill

South Breakwater
Knuckle Light 15m
Occ 10s WR sectors
W239°-059° 15M
R059°-239° 13M

Dover Cas
ABB

South
Breakwater
E end light
on mast
F orange 4M

DOVER E entrance

Signal station

3 radio trs ACC

Bldg Flared roof BBC

RED

WHITE

DOVER

TOP

SW Goodwin Buoys (S)

S Goodwin LV
12m GpFl (2) 30s 25M
Dia (2) 60s

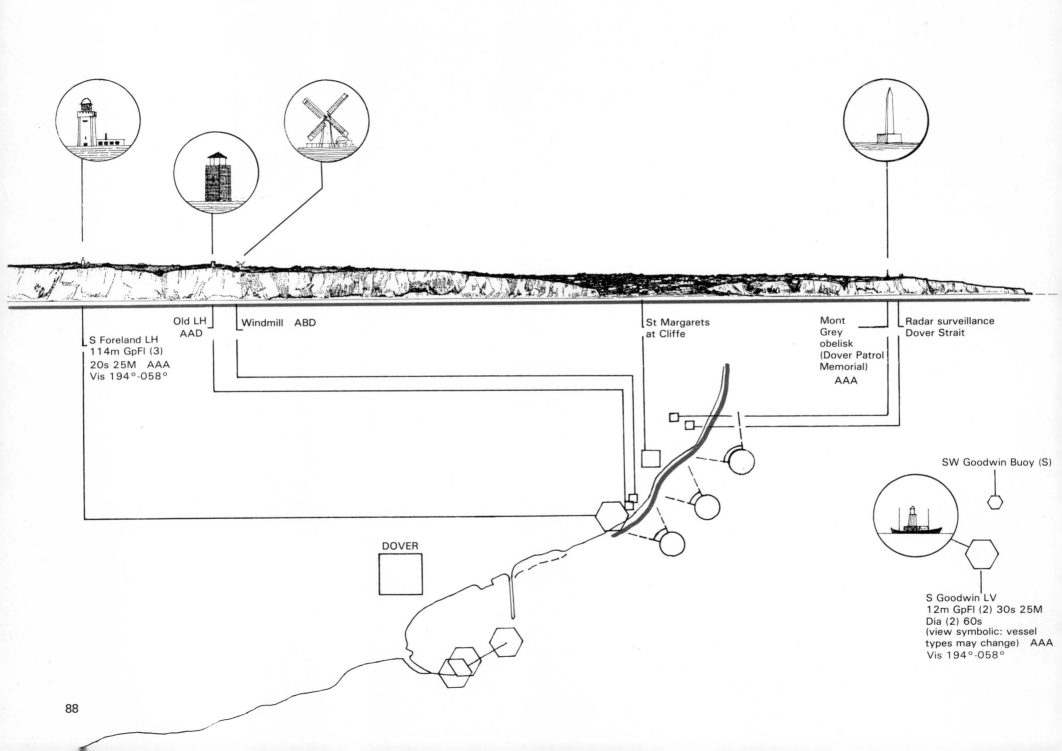

S Foreland LH
114m GpFl (3)
20s 25M   AAA
Vis 194°-058°

Old LH
AAD

Windmill   ABD

St Margarets
at Cliffe

Mont
Grey
obelisk
(Dover Patrol
Memorial)
   AAA

Radar surveillance
Dover Strait

DOVER

SW Goodwin Buoy (S)

S Goodwin LV
12m GpFl (2) 30s 25M
Dia (2) 60s
(view symbolic: vessel
types may change)   AAA
Vis 194°-058°